Retire with Confidence

Mastering Insurance for Long-Term Security

By
Nathan Venture, D

To You,

You've earned it!

Table of Contents

Introduction: The Pillars of a Secure Retirement 1

Chapter 1: Insurance Essentials for Retirement 5
Understanding Insurance Types and Terms 5
Evaluating Your Insurance Needs 8

Chapter 2: Life Insurance Strategies for Retirees 12
Term vs. Permanent Life Insurance in Retirement 12
Using Life Insurance for Estate Planning 15

Chapter 3: Annuities and Retirement Income 19
Types of Annuities and Their Benefits 19
Incorporating Annuities into Your Retirement Plan 22

Chapter 4: Long-Term Care Insurance: Preparing for Medical
Expenses 26
Understanding Long-Term Care Coverage 26
How to Choose the Right Long-Term Care Policy 29

Chapter 5: Health Insurance Options for Retirees 33
Medicare and Supplemental Policies 33
Alternatives to Traditional Health Insurance 37

Chapter 6: Disability Insurance to Protect Your Retirement 41
Long-Term Disability Insurance Explained 41
Integrating Disability Insurance with Other Retirement Income
Sources 44

Chapter 7: Liability Insurance in Retirement 48
Umbrella Policies for Comprehensive Protection 48

Assessing Your Liability Risks 51

Chapter 8: Property and Casualty Insurance for Retirees.................. 55
Homeowners and Auto Insurance Considerations 55
Insurance for Other Assets and Properties 58

Chapter 9: The Role of Social Security in Retirement Planning........ 62
Maximizing Social Security Benefits 62
Coordinating Social Security with Other Retirement Income....... 65

Chapter 10: Investment Strategies Integrated with Insurance............ 69
Balancing Risk with Insurance-Backed Investments....................... 69
Diversification with Insurance Products 72

Chapter 11: Tax Considerations for Insurance in Retirement........... 77
Tax Advantages of Insurance Policies... 77
Navigating the Tax Implications of Retirement Distributions 80

Chapter 12: A Guide to Estate Planning with Insurance.................... 84
Using Insurance Products to Create a Legacy 84
Trusts and Insurance: Protecting Your Estate for Future
Generations 88

Chapter 13: Ensuring a Secure and Sustainable Retirement.............. 91

Glossary of Insurance Terms for Easy Reference 95

Appendix A: Insurance Planning Worksheets and Checklists............ 99

Introduction:
The Pillars of a Secure Retirement

Planning for retirement isn't just about amassing a substantial nest egg; it's about constructing a resilient financial framework that will safeguard your well-being and aspirations throughout your golden years. For many, the myriad options available for retirement planning can seem overwhelming. This book aims to demystify one critical component of that puzzle: insurance products. The goal is to guide you in leveraging these products effectively so that your retirement is not just secure but also enriching and worry-free.

Insurance isn't just a rainy-day fund or a safeguard against unforeseen events. When integrated thoughtfully, it can become a cornerstone of a holistic retirement plan. Each chapter in this book will elucidate different types of insurance products and their strategic applications, creating a comprehensive guide to fortifying your financial future.

Imagine your retirement plan as a cathedral. Each insurance product serves as a vital pillar that supports the overall structure. Without one, the entire edifice could become unstable. Understanding these pillars—life insurance, annuities, long-term care insurance, health insurance, disability insurance, liability insurance, and property and casualty insurance—is essential for constructing a secure foundation for your retirement.

Let's begin by highlighting why insurance is indispensable in retirement planning. First and foremost, insurance mitigates risk. We all face uncertainties, from health crises to market volatility. Insurance products act as a financial cushion, helping you weather such storms without derailing your retirement goals. This risk mitigation allows you to enjoy a stable and predictable income stream, turning your focus to what truly matters: living your life to the fullest.

Another vital aspect is the flexibility that insurance products bring to the table. Whether it's managing ongoing medical expenses or providing for loved ones after you're gone, insurance can be tailored to meet your unique needs and aspirations. It can serve as both a protective shield and a financial tool that adapts as your circumstances evolve.

Furthermore, insurance can offer notable tax advantages, adding an extra layer of financial efficiency to your retirement plan. By understanding the tax implications, you can make more informed decisions that ultimately maximize your retirement income and leave a lasting legacy for future generations.

Take, for instance, the role of life insurance. Many people think of life insurance merely as a way to provide for dependents after one's death. However, it can be a powerful instrument in estate planning, ensuring that your heirs aren't burdened with hefty tax bills. It can also serve as a vehicle for charitable donations, aligning with your values and passions.

Annuities, on the other hand, offer the promise of a steady income stream, thereby eliminating the fear of outliving your savings. They can be customized to suit your needs, whether you prefer a fixed income or one that adjusts for inflation. Understanding the different types and their respective benefits will empower you to incorporate this dependable income source into your broader strategy.

Health insurance often becomes more complex as you age, but its importance can't be overstated. Medicare and supplemental policies are critical to managing medical expenses, but they're not your only options. Exploring alternatives can open doors to personalized solutions that better serve your needs.

Long-term care insurance is another critical component, addressing the potential high costs of extended medical and personal care. As people live longer, the likelihood of requiring long-term care increases, making this type of insurance not just beneficial but essential for preserving your savings.

Disability insurance provides another layer of protection, ensuring that you have a steady income even if you're unable to work due to illness or injury. Integrating disability insurance with other income sources can create a safety net that preserves your quality of life.

Liability insurance, including umbrella policies, offers comprehensive protection against lawsuits and claims. This type of coverage is particularly crucial as you accumulate assets and enjoy a more comfortable lifestyle. It shields your hard-earned savings from unforeseen legal challenges.

Property and casualty insurance, from homeowners to auto insurance, also play a crucial role in protecting your assets. Understanding the nuances of each can help you make informed decisions that safeguard your investments and lifestyle.

By breaking down each type of insurance, examining their benefits, and exploring strategies to integrate them into your retirement plan, this book will serve as your compass on the intricate journey of retirement planning. The forthcoming chapters offer a wealth of information tailored to help you create a robust, dynamic, and secure retirement strategy.

Before we delve into the specifics of each insurance type, take a moment to consider what a secure retirement means to you. Whether it's pursuing hobbies, traveling, or spending more time with family, your retirement goals should shape your strategy. As you navigate through this book, keep those aspirations in mind, allowing them to guide your choices and decisions.

In the end, the true value of a secure retirement lies in the peace of mind it brings. With a well-constructed plan that integrates the right insurance products, you gain the freedom to live your life on your terms, knowing that you're protected against uncertainties. So, let's embark on this journey together, building the pillars that will support not just a secure retirement, but a fulfilling and vibrant future.

Welcome to the journey of constructing your secure retirement. With each chapter, we'll navigate the landscape of insurance products, uncovering the possibilities and strategies that will empower you to achieve long-term financial security and peace of mind. Let's get started.

Chapter 1:
Insurance Essentials for Retirement

As you start your journey toward a secure retirement, understanding the essentials of insurance is your first crucial step. Insurance is more than just a safety net; it's a strategic tool that can ensure financial stability and peace of mind throughout your golden years. Knowing the basic types of insurance available and key terms will empower you to make informed decisions based on your unique needs. From life insurance to annuities, these products offer tailored solutions designed to protect your assets, provide a steady income, and cover unforeseen expenses. Dive in with an intent to learn, and you'll find that insurance, when utilized effectively, can be your most reliable ally in crafting a future that not only meets your financial goals but surpasses them.

Understanding Insurance Types and Terms

Understanding Insurance Types and Terms is crucial to mastering the art of using insurance products for a secure and strategic retirement plan. At its core, insurance is about risk management. Different types of insurance protect against different risks, offering financial security amid life's uncertainties. But navigating the landscape of insurance can be confusing, with its myriad of terms and complex policy structures. This section will demystify it all.

Insurance isn't a one-size-fits-all solution; each type of insurance serves a unique purpose. Typically, insurance can be segmented into life insurance, health insurance, long-term care insurance, disability insurance, liability insurance, and property and casualty insurance. Each of these types provides coverage for specific aspects of life, contributing to an overall secure and comprehensive retirement plan.

Life insurance products, such as term and permanent insurance, offer financial protection for your beneficiaries upon your passing. Term insurance covers a specified period, while permanent insurance provides lifetime coverage along with a cash value component. Understanding these differences is key to choosing the right type of life insurance for your needs.

Health insurance plays a pivotal role in protecting against exorbitant medical expenses. For retirees, this often means navigating Medicare and supplemental policies, but it can also include private health insurance options. Each policy type comes with its own set of terms and coverage limitations, which you'll need to fully understand to make informed choices.

When it comes to long-term care insurance, it's all about planning ahead for future healthcare needs. Long-term care policies cover the costs of extended medical care, either in-home or in specialized facilities. This type of coverage is essential for those looking to protect their retirement savings from being depleted by long-term care costs.

Disability insurance ensures that you'll continue to receive an income if you're unable to work due to illness or injury. Understanding the terms of short-term versus long-term disability insurance can help you decide which coverage best protects your financial stability during retirement.

Liability insurance, including umbrella policies, provides an additional layer of protection against potential lawsuits and claims. This type of coverage is invaluable for safeguarding your assets and ensuring that unexpected legal costs don't derail your retirement plans.

Property and casualty insurance, often encompassing homeowners and auto insurance, protects your physical assets. In retirement, you may need to adjust your coverage to account for changes in your lifestyle and residence, ensuring that your assets remain protected.

Now, let's delve into some of the common terms you'll encounter in insurance policies. Terms like "premium," "deductible," "benefit," "cash value," and "claim" are ubiquitous in the insurance world. The premium is the amount you pay for your insurance policy, usually on a monthly or annual basis. The deductible is the amount you're responsible for before your insurance kicks in. The benefit is the payout you receive from your policy. Cash value refers to the savings component found in some life insurance policies. A claim is a request made to your insurance company for payment of benefits.

Another crucial term is "underwriting". This process determines whether an insurance company will issue a policy to a potential policyholder and at what premium level. Underwriters assess risk based on your health, age, occupation, and other factors. Understanding underwriting is important because it affects your eligibility and the cost of your insurance.

Additionally, "beneficiary" is a significant term, especially in life insurance. This is the person or entity you designate to receive the policy's benefit upon your passing. Designating the right beneficiaries is critical for ensuring your loved ones are financially protected.

Other terms to be aware of include "renewal," "exclusion," and "rider." Renewal refers to continuing your policy after its term ends, often requiring an assessment of your current risk status. Exclusions are specific conditions or circumstances not covered by your policy. Riders are additional provisions or amendments that you can add to your basic policy for extra coverage.

It's also useful to acquaint yourself with "policyholder" rights and obligations. As a policyholder, you're entitled to certain benefits and protections but also have responsibilities, such as providing accurate information and paying your premiums on time. Being clear on these aspects ensures a smoother relationship with your insurer.

Understanding insurance types and terms involves grasping the basics and recognizing how different types of insurance can integrate to form a robust retirement strategy. It's about making informed choices that align with your financial goals and personal circumstances.

As you move forward in exploring other chapters and sections of this book, remember that knowledge is power. Being well-versed in insurance basics is the first step toward leveraging these products for securing a stable and prosperous retirement. So, delve deeper, equip yourself with the right information, and take confident strides toward a financially secure future.

Your journey through the intricacies of insurance will not only safeguard your retirement but also provide peace of mind, knowing that you're prepared for whatever life throws your way. Stay informed, stay protected, and let your retirement be as serene and carefree as you've always envisioned.

Evaluating Your Insurance Needs

Evaluating Your Insurance Needs an essential step in crafting a well-rounded retirement plan. This process is all about assessing your current financial situation, understanding potential risks, and determining the types and amounts of insurance that will provide the security you need. You can't afford to ignore this; it forms the backbone of a resilient retirement strategy.

First, you should start with a thorough inventory of your existing assets, liabilities, income, and expenses. What do you own? What do you owe? What income streams do you have now, and what do you expect in retirement? Jot all this down; it's your starting point. This clear financial picture will help in pinpointing where insurance can fill in gaps.

Next, it's crucial to consider your life expectancy and health. While nobody can predict the future with certainty, actuarial tables and your personal health history can provide some guidance. If longevity runs in your family, you might need to plan for a longer retirement and consider insurance products like long-term care insurance more seriously.

Think about your family's financial needs, too. Ask yourself, "If something happened to me, would my family be financially secure?" Life insurance can provide peace of mind, knowing your loved ones won't face financial strain in your absence. It's not just about covering funeral expenses; it's about replacing lost income and helping your family maintain their standard of living.

Another factor is your risk tolerance. Are you the kind of person who prefers to shelter from potential storms, or are you comfortable taking some risks? Your answer can influence whether you opt for basic coverage or comprehensive policies with higher premiums but broader protections. Your risk tolerance intertwines with your overall financial strategy, affecting your investment choices and how insurance fits into your plan.

When evaluating your insurance needs, you should also consider the potential for inflation. Inflation can erode your purchasing power over time, making it crucial to opt for policies that have provisions to keep up with rising costs. For instance, look for long-term care policies with inflation protection riders. Without this, you might find the benefits insufficient at the time you actually need them.

Liability risks are another important area to evaluate. As you move into retirement, your risk profile changes. You might travel more, volunteer, or even start a side business. Each of these activities could expose you to different kinds of liabilities. An umbrella policy might be a worthwhile consideration to protect against large, unexpected claims that could deplete your retirement savings.

Don't overlook property-related insurance needs, either. Many retirees downsize or relocate, altering their insurance requirements in the process. Ensure that any new home is adequately insured, and consider the potential need for flood or earthquake insurance, depending on your new location. Also, updating auto insurance to reflect decreased usage or even increased vehicle value if you buy a new car can make a big difference.

Your employment status changes in retirement, which can also affect your insurance needs. While employed, you might have had life, health, and disability insurance through your employer. As you transition to retirement, you need to replace or supplement these with individually purchased policies. Understanding these shifts and planning ahead can prevent coverage gaps.

Reviewing your insurance needs isn't a one-time task. Your circumstances and the external environment can change, necessitating periodic reassessments. Set a schedule, maybe annually or bi-annually, to review your coverage. Doing so ensures you remain adequately protected as your life and the world around you evolve.

Cost is, of course, a major consideration. Insurance premiums can be a significant expense, particularly on a fixed retirement income. Therefore, it's vital to shop around and compare different policies. Look at both the premiums and the benefits offered to ensure value for money. Bundling policies can sometimes result in discounts, so explore integrated options.

Additionally, it's wise to consult with financial advisors and insurance professionals. They can offer insights you might not have considered and provide tailored advice based on their expertise. What works for someone else may not work for you, so personalized guidance is incredibly valuable in this domain.

Ultimately, evaluating your insurance needs is about matching your personal circumstances with the right products. It's like assembling a puzzle where each piece—be it life, health, long-term care, or liability insurance—must fit perfectly to complete the picture of your secure retirement.

Embrace this process with an open mind and a willingness to explore all options. A thoughtful evaluation ensures you're not just protected against the expected but are also resilient against unforeseen challenges. It's an investment in your peace of mind and a cornerstone of your retirement strategy.

By taking these steps to evaluate and plan, you can transform what might seem like daunting insurance decisions into a coherent strategy that aligns with your retirement dreams. Your future self will thank you for the diligence and foresight you've displayed today.

Chapter 2:
Life Insurance Strategies for Retirees

As you transition into retirement, life insurance remains a vital component of your financial strategy, offering invaluable flexibility and security. Whether it's choosing between term and permanent life insurance or leveraging policies for estate planning, each option demands a keen understanding of both your current needs and future goals. Term life insurance can provide a cost-effective way to cover immediate obligations, while permanent life insurance offers lifelong protection and can accumulate cash value over time. This cash value can serve as a financial cushion or be used to meet specific legacy objectives, such as funding a trust or supporting charitable causes. Moreover, effective use of life insurance in estate planning can mitigate potential tax burdens, ensuring that more of your assets are passed on to your heirs. So, whether you aim to safeguard your spouse's financial stability, manage estate taxes, or leave a lasting legacy, thoughtfully chosen life insurance strategies can seamlessly integrate with your broader retirement plan, laying a solid foundation for a secure and fulfilling retired life.

Term vs. Permanent Life Insurance in Retirement

This serves as the foundation upon which many strategic retirement plans are built. When you're planning for a secure and comfortable retirement, life insurance can play a crucial role in ensuring financial stability and peace of mind. Whether you choose term or permanent life insurance depends on your specific needs, goals, and circumstances.

It's essential to start by understanding the fundamental differences between term and permanent life insurance. Term life insurance provides coverage for a specified period, typically ranging from 10 to 30 years. Once the term expires, the insurance coverage ends unless it's renewed or converted to a permanent policy. On the other hand, permanent life insurance, which includes whole life and universal life, covers you for your entire life as long as premiums are paid.

When contemplating the integration of term versus permanent life insurance in retirement, consider your primary objective. Term life insurance is typically more affordable initially, making it appealing if your focus is to cover specific obligations like paying off a mortgage, funding your children's education, or replacing lost income during your working years. However, in retirement, these needs often diminish or disappear altogether.

For retirees, the appeal of permanent life insurance lies in its lifelong coverage and additional benefits. One of the significant advantages is the cash value component, which grows over time and can be accessed if needed. This feature can serve as a supplementary income source, provide emergency funds, or even be used to cover long-term care expenses.

Another crucial factor is estate planning. Permanent life insurance can be an effective tool for creating a financial legacy. The death benefit from a permanent policy can help cover estate taxes, debts, and other final expenses, ensuring that your loved ones aren't burdened with unforeseen costs. Additionally, it can facilitate the smooth transfer of wealth to your heirs or favorite charities.

It's essential to assess your health status before deciding between term and permanent life insurance. Permanent policies tend to be more accommodating for those with health issues, allowing you to secure coverage even if term insurance might be prohibitively expensive or unavailable. On the flip side, if you're in excellent health and primarily need coverage for a finite period, term insurance might still be a viable option.

When evaluating life insurance needs in retirement, consider your overall financial portfolio. If you have ample retirement savings, pensions, Social Security benefits, and no dependents relying on your income, you might lean towards minimal coverage. However, if your retirement assets are anticipated to fall short of your needs or if you have dependent beneficiaries, more robust insurance coverage may be warranted.

Cost is a substantial consideration. While term life insurance is generally more cost-effective initially, rely on permanent insurance if you're concerned about maintaining coverage well into your later years. Permanent policies, although more expensive, offer the assurance of continuous coverage and the added benefit of cash value accumulation.

Another key point is the flexibility of the insurance products. Universal life insurance, a subtype of permanent insurance, offers flexible premium payments and death benefits, allowing you to adjust your policy as your financial situation changes over time. This adaptability can be particularly beneficial during retirement when income streams may fluctuate.

Tax considerations can also not be overlooked. The cash value growth in permanent life insurance policies is tax-deferred, and the death benefits are generally paid out tax-free. These tax advantages make permanent life insurance an attractive option for wealth accumulation and preservation.

Let's not forget the emotional aspect. Peace of mind plays a vital role in retirement planning. Knowing that you have a permanent life insurance policy in place can eliminate worries about coverage lapsing when you might need it most, providing a sense of security for both you and your loved ones.

If you're unsure which route to take, you might consider a hybrid approach. Some retirees opt for a blend of term and permanent life insurance, leveraging the affordability of term insurance for short-term needs while securing the lifelong benefits of permanent insurance.

As you venture deeper into your retirement planning journey, keep in mind that life insurance needs are highly individualized. What works for one person might not be suitable for another. A thorough assessment of your financial situation, goals, health, and family dynamics is imperative in making an informed decision.

Engaging with a financial advisor who specializes in retirement planning can be invaluable. They can provide personalized recommendations and help you navigate the complexities of term and permanent life insurance, ensuring that your retirement strategy aligns with your long-term objectives.

Term vs. Permanent Life Insurance in Retirement is more than just a choice; it's a pivotal decision that impacts your financial strategy and peace of mind. Take the time to evaluate your unique needs, seek professional guidance, and make informed choices that contribute to a secure and fulfilling retirement.

Using Life Insurance for Estate Planning

Using Life Insurance for Estate Planning has long been a strategic facet of effective retirement planning. It's not just about ensuring your family has a financial cushion; it's about controlling how your assets are managed and distributed after you've passed on. By incorporating life insurance within your estate planning, you're setting up mechanisms that can provide not only liquidity but also significant tax advantages. In this section, we'll detail how life insurance can be an indispensable tool for protecting your estate and ensuring your legacy.

When considering *life insurance for estate planning*, one of the first benefits that come to mind is the provision of immediate funds upon your death. Life insurance policies typically pay out relatively quickly, providing instant liquidity that can be crucial for covering estate taxes, debts, and other obligations. This is particularly beneficial if most of your assets are tied up in non-liquid investments like real estate or business interests. Your heirs won't have to scramble to sell assets at less-than-ideal times just to cover immediate costs.

The death benefit from a life insurance policy is generally income tax-free to your beneficiaries. This significant perk can't be overstated when you're trying to pass along as much as possible to your heirs. Essentially, you're providing them with a tax-free sum that can help them manage various expenses, and even invest for their future without having to worry about the IRS taking a chunk out of it.

Another compelling feature of life insurance in estate planning is its ability to equalize inheritance among heirs. Let's say you have a business or real estate property you want to leave to one child, but you also want to ensure your other children get an equivalent value. You can use a life insurance policy to designate a cash value to those other children, thereby maintaining fairness and reducing the potential for family disputes.

There are also significant estate tax considerations when using life insurance for estate planning. The funds from a life insurance policy can be used to pay estate taxes, reducing the need to liquidate other assets that might be more valuable or generate ongoing income. This becomes especially critical for larger estates that exceed the federal estate tax exemption limits or if you reside in states with their own estate or inheritance taxes.

Placing a life insurance policy in an irrevocable life insurance trust (ILIT) can further enhance its estate planning benefits. By transferring ownership of the policy to an ILIT, you can potentially remove the life insurance proceeds from your taxable estate, ensuring that they're out of reach of creditors and estate tax liabilities. The trust can then manage and distribute the funds according to your wishes, providing even more control and protection for your heirs.

The specific type of life insurance you choose can also have varying impacts on your estate plan. Whole life or universal life policies offer the added benefit of building cash value that you can tap into if needed during your lifetime. This cash value can be a valuable resource for unexpected expenses or opportunities, providing another layer of financial security.

On the other hand, term life insurance can be a cost-effective way to provide significant death benefits if you're primarily focused on covering short-term needs such as mortgages or education costs. However, its lack of cash value means it won't offer the same long-term benefits as permanent insurance policies. Nevertheless, it can be a critical component depending on your specific circumstances and retirement planning goals.

It's also essential to regularly review and update your life insurance policies and beneficiaries as part of your estate planning effort. Life events such as marriage, divorce, the birth of children, or the death of beneficiaries can significantly impact your estate plan. Keeping your policies current ensures that your intentions are accurately reflected and that your loved ones are protected in the way you envisioned.

Another strategic use of life insurance in estate planning is funding buy-sell agreements for business owners. If you own a business, a life insurance policy can provide the funds necessary for your business partners to buy out your share upon your death. This ensures business continuity and provides your heirs with the liquidity they need without having to manage the complexities of an ongoing business.

The ability to leverage life insurance for charitable giving also makes it a powerful estate planning tool. You can designate a charity as a beneficiary of your policy, allowing you to leave a lasting legacy to a cause close to your heart. This not only benefits the charity but can also provide your estate with a charitable deduction, potentially lowering the overall tax burden.

It's worth noting that life insurance can also protect against the unexpected. By having a policy in place, you provide a safety net for your heirs that can help them navigate the financial burdens that arise from losing you. This security can be instrumental in helping them maintain their standard of living and pursue their goals without undue financial strain.

The motivational aspect of using life insurance for estate planning is evident in the profound peace of mind it offers. Knowing that your loved ones will be taken care of, that your assets will be managed according to your wishes, and that your legacy will be preserved, allows you to enjoy your retirement more fully. You have the assurance that you have put in place solid, strategic measures to protect what matters most.

In conclusion, life insurance is not merely a tool for financial protection; it is a cornerstone of comprehensive estate planning. As you navigate the intricacies of retirement planning, leveraging life insurance thoughtfully can provide extensive benefits, from tax advantages and liquidity to equalizing inheritances and supporting charitable causes. It ensures that you leave behind a well-organized, financially sound legacy for your loved ones, fulfilling your final wishes while providing them with continued security.

Chapter 3:
Annuities and Retirement Income

Transitioning from the cornerstone concepts of life insurance, we dive into annuities—a pivotal instrument in ensuring a steady income stream during retirement. Think of annuities as your personal pension plan, tailored to bridge the gap between your working years and the golden years ahead. They offer the stability of guaranteed payments and can be meticulously structured to fit your needs, whether you're aiming for lifelong payouts or seeking income over a specific period. Integrating annuities into your retirement plan is about crafting financial predictability, where the fog of uncertainty lifts to reveal a clear path towards sustained financial security. By understanding and leveraging the variety of annuity products available, you can strategically design a retirement income that's resilient against market fluctuations and longevity risks, empowering you to enjoy life's adventures with unshakable confidence.

Types of Annuities and Their Benefits

This topic moves us to unravel a key component of a sturdy retirement plan. At its core, an annuity is a financial product that offers a fixed stream of payments to an individual, primarily used as an income stream for retirees. The versatility of annuities makes them a valuable tool in retirement planning, offering various types tailored to meet different financial goals and risk appetites.

Firstly, let's talk about *fixed annuities*. A fixed annuity provides regular, guaranteed payments, making them ideal for those who seek stability and predictability. The insurance company guarantees a minimum rate of return on your investment, protecting your principal from market fluctuations. For retirees, this peace of mind can be invaluable, knowing that each payment will be consistent regardless of economic conditions outside.

In contrast, *variable annuities* offer the potential for higher returns, albeit with added risk. With variable annuities, your money is invested in sub-accounts, which are similar to mutual funds, and your payouts depend on the performance of these investments. This provides an opportunity for growth that fixed annuities don't afford but comes with the risk that your payments could decrease if the market performs poorly. Variable annuities are suitable for those who have a higher risk tolerance and are looking for potential growth over time.

Moreover, *indexed annuities* strike a balance between fixed and variable annuities. These provide a return that's linked to a market index, such as the S&P 500, allowing for growth potential while also offering a guaranteed minimum return. This hybrid nature makes indexed annuities appealing to those who want to take advantage of market gains without exposing their entire investment to market risks.

Then we have *immediate annuities*, which start paying out almost immediately after a lump sum is paid into the annuity. This can be a practical choice for individuals who have a significant amount of money saved and are ready to begin receiving income right away. Immediate annuities are particularly beneficial for new retirees who need to quickly convert their savings into a reliable stream of income.

For those keen on planning long term, *deferred annuities* can be a strategic choice. Deferred annuities allow your money to grow tax-deferred until you start withdrawing funds, typically many years in the future. This type is perfect for individuals who have other income sources or savings strategies in place for the initial years of retirement and wish to supplement their income later on.

One key benefit of annuities, regardless of type, is the option for *lifetime income*. Many annuities offer a lifetime income option, which ensures that you won't outlive your savings. This provides retirees with the security of knowing they will have a steady income stream for life, helping to maintain their standard of living and cover essential expenses.

Besides income stability, another compelling advantage is *tax deferral*. The money invested in an annuity grows tax-deferred until it is withdrawn, meaning you won't pay taxes on the growth until you start receiving payments. This can be particularly advantageous in managing your tax burden in retirement, providing you the ability to strategize withdrawals during low tax years.

Annuities also offer *customizable features* through various riders, which can be added to tailor the annuity to better match personal needs. For instance, a cost-of-living adjustment (COLA) rider can help your payments keep pace with inflation, ensuring your income doesn't lose purchasing power over time. Death benefit riders can ensure that your remaining funds are passed on to beneficiaries, providing peace of mind and legacy planning.

For those concerned about *long-term care*, some annuities offer long-term care riders that can help cover future medical and care expenses. This dual-functionality can be a lifesaver as healthcare costs continue to rise, providing an added layer of financial protection.

One often understated benefit is the *legacy potential* of annuities. By using certain riders or structuring your annuity appropriately, you can ensure that your remaining funds are passed on to your beneficiaries in a tax-efficient manner. This allows you to not only secure your own financial future but also leave a lasting impact on your loved ones.

Furthermore, annuities can serve as a tool for *financial discipline*. By converting a lump sum into periodic payments, an annuity can help prevent overspending and ensure that funds are available throughout retirement. This can be especially beneficial for those who are concerned about managing their savings effectively and resisting the temptation to spend too quickly.

Combining different types of annuities can also be strategically advantageous. For example, you could start with an immediate annuity to cover current expenses and add a deferred annuity to ensure future income. This approach allows you to benefit from the strengths of different annuity types while mitigating their individual weaknesses.

To sum up, understanding the various types of annuities and their specific benefits can significantly enhance your retirement planning. Whether you prioritize stability, growth potential, or a combination of both, there's an annuity designed to meet your needs. By incorporating well-chosen annuities into your retirement strategy, you can ensure a steady income stream and enjoy peace of mind no matter what the future holds.

The next section will delve into how to effectively incorporate annuities into your overall retirement plan, enhancing your financial security and ensuring a comfortable retirement.

Incorporating Annuities into Your Retirement Plan

Incorporating Annuities into Your Retirement Plan is a critical step in ensuring your financial security throughout your golden years. While the term "annuity" might initially sound complex or daunting, it's essentially about securing a steady stream of income, akin to receiving a paycheck during retirement. Let's dive into how you can make these powerful financial instruments work for you.

An element that sets annuities apart from other investment vehicles is their ability to provide guaranteed income. When you purchase an annuity, you're essentially buying a promise from an insurance company that they'll pay you a certain amount of money periodically, either for a fixed period or for as long as you live. Think of it as creating your own personal pension plan.

One of the initial considerations when incorporating annuities into your retirement plan is understanding the different types available. Whether you're considering a fixed, variable, immediate, or deferred annuity, each has unique attributes tailored to meet diverse financial needs and risk appetites. Fixed annuities, for instance, offer guaranteed payouts, making them an excellent choice for risk-averse individuals.

Variable annuities, on the other hand, offer the potential for higher returns since they are linked to the performance of investment portfolios. However, they also come with greater risk. This choice is ideal if you're looking to balance the certainty of income with the potential for growth, much like diversifying your investment portfolio.

Immediate annuities start paying out almost immediately after you make a lump-sum payment. This makes them suitable for individuals who are either at or close to retirement age and wish to convert their savings into an income stream. On the flip side, deferred annuities allow your money to grow tax-deferred until you're ready to start receiving payments. This makes them an excellent option for those planning ahead.

Timing is another crucial factor to consider. Deciding when to begin receiving annuity payments can have a significant impact on your overall financial health. Starting earlier might offer immediate financial security, but waiting a few years can often result in larger payouts. Evaluate your retirement timeline and existing financial commitments carefully to make an informed decision.

Customizing your annuity is another aspect that can make this financial tool incredibly powerful. Many annuities come with optional riders that can address specific needs, such as inflation protection, guaranteed minimum income benefits, or even long-term care provisions. While these additional features might increase the cost, they can offer invaluable peace of mind.

Furthermore, it's not just about the money you'll get each month. Integrating annuities into the broader context of your retirement plan can help you manage risks more effectively. For example, annuity income can serve as a hedge against market volatility, providing a stable financial foundation regardless of economic conditions.

The interaction between annuities and other retirement income sources, such as Social Security, pensions, and investment withdrawals, is also critical. Aim for a balanced income strategy to ensure you aren't solely relying on one source. This diversified approach can offer more financial stability and increase your overall retirement security.

Another aspect worth exploring is the tax implications. The payouts from different types of annuities may have varying tax treatments. Understanding these can let you maximize your income while managing your tax liabilities efficiently. Specialized advice from a tax consultant familiar with retirement planning can be an asset here.

Choosing the right insurance provider to purchase your annuity from is also pivotal. Research the financial health, customer service reputation, and product offerings of potential insurance companies. Given that you're entrusting them with a significant portion of your retirement savings, ensure they have a strong track record of fulfilling their commitments.

Comparing quotes from different providers can help you secure the best rates and features for your needs. Take your time to read the fine print and understand all terms and conditions. It's always better to ask questions upfront than to face complications later on.

Educating yourself is perhaps one of the most potent strategies you have. The more knowledgeable you are about annuities and how they fit into your retirement plan, the more empowered and confident you'll be in making decisions that safeguard your financial future.

Lastly, don't overlook the importance of reviewing and adjusting your annuity strategy as time goes on. Life circumstances, financial goals, and market conditions may change. Regularly reassessing your plan can help you stay on track and make necessary adjustments to keep everything aligned with your long-term objectives.

To sum up, incorporating annuities into your retirement plan requires careful consideration and strategic planning. By understanding your needs, exploring your options, and keeping an eye on the long-term benefits, you can set the foundation for a secure and fulfilling retirement.

Chapter 4:
Long-Term Care Insurance:
Preparing for Medical Expenses

As we navigate the labyrinth of retirement planning, one crucial piece often overlooked is long-term care insurance. This pivotal coverage can significantly ease the burden of potentially astronomical medical expenses later in life, ensuring that your hard-earned savings aren't wiped out by unforeseen health issues. Long-term care insurance covers a variety of services, from in-home healthcare to assisted living and nursing home facilities, providing peace of mind that you and your loved ones will be well-cared for. By integrating this into your retirement strategy, you're not just planning for today but safeguarding your financial future against the unpredictable nature of aging. Remember, the goal here is not merely survival—it's thriving, by securing comprehensive protection for all stages of your life. So, take a proactive approach now to navigate the maze of options available and choose a policy that aligns with your healthcare needs and long-term financial goals.

Understanding Long-Term Care Coverage

Understanding Long-Term Care Coverage is an essential step in ensuring that your retirement plan covers all bases. Many people overlook long-term care (LTC) coverage, thinking it's something they'll never need. But the reality is, a significant number of us will require some form of long-term care in our later years, whether it's due to aging, chronic illness, or disability. Understanding what LTC coverage entails can be a game-changer for your financial security.

Long-term care coverage is distinct from traditional health insurance and Medicare. While health insurance and Medicare typically cover short-term medical needs and hospitalization, LTC insurance is designed to cover services that assist with daily living activities over an extended period. These services include help with bathing, dressing, eating, and more.

One of the first things to realize about LTC coverage is its broad scope. It can cover care provided in various settings such as your home, an assisted living facility, a nursing home, or an adult day care center. This flexibility ensures that you have options tailored to your personal preferences and needs.

When considering long-term care insurance, it's crucial to understand the types of care covered. Typically, LTC policies provide coverage for three main types of care: personal care, skilled nursing care, and custodial care. Personal care deals with assistance in daily activities, skilled nursing care involves medical services provided by licensed professionals, and custodial care focuses on non-medical support.

The cost of long-term care can be staggering without insurance. The average annual cost for a private room in a nursing home can surpass $100,000, and even in-home care costs can quickly add up. Without adequate coverage, these expenses can deplete your retirement savings rapidly, leaving you vulnerable. Investing in LTC insurance helps mitigate these risks by providing financial support when you need it most.

To effectively utilize LTC coverage, start by understanding the elimination period, which functions similarly to a deductible but in terms of time. This period ranges from 30 to 90 days, during which you'll cover costs out-of-pocket before the policy starts to pay. Choosing a longer elimination period can lower your premiums but requires careful financial planning to cover interim expenses.

Another critical element is the benefit period, which dictates how long the insurer will cover your care once you qualify. Options generally range from two years to a lifetime. While longer benefit periods offer more comprehensive coverage, they come with higher premiums. Assessing your family history and personal health can guide you in selecting the appropriate benefit period.

You should also pay close attention to the daily benefit amount, which is the maximum amount the policy will pay for your care each day. Balancing your daily benefit with anticipated costs in your preferred care setting ensures that you won't face significant out-of-pocket expenses down the line.

Inflation protection is another essential feature to consider. Healthcare and care facility costs rise over time, and what seems like adequate coverage today may not suffice in the future. Inflation riders adjust your benefits to keep pace with rising costs, offering a valuable safeguard for the longevity of your coverage.

Understanding policy triggers is paramount as well. These triggers determine when you become eligible to start receiving benefits. Usually, benefits kick in when you can't perform two out of six activities of daily living (ADLs) like bathing, dressing, or eating. Cognitive impairments such as Alzheimer's disease also commonly trigger benefits.

Transparency in reading and understanding your policy details cannot be overemphasized. Each LTC policy can be uniquely structured with different exclusions, benefits, and terms. Taking the time to thoroughly review and understand these nuances ensures that there are no surprises when you need to file a claim.

While premiums for LTC insurance can be high, there are strategies to manage costs. For instance, purchasing a policy at a younger age usually results in lower premiums. Additionally, some policies offer shared care options for couples, allowing them to pool benefits and reduce overall costs.

Long-term care partnerships, available in many states, offer another cost management strategy. These partnerships enable policyholders to protect a portion of their assets if they exhaust their insurance benefits and then need to apply for Medicaid. This dual approach can provide comprehensive financial security.

The peace of mind that comes with having a long-term care policy cannot be overstated. It allows you and your loved ones to focus on quality time together instead of being burdened by mounting care expenses. Additionally, it provides the freedom to choose the type of care and setting that aligns with your personal preferences.

As you continue your journey in understanding and implementing insurance products for retirement, remember that long-term care coverage is a critical component. It not only protects your financial well-being but also ensures that you have access to the care you may need, preserving your independence and dignity as you age.

How to Choose the Right Long-Term Care Policy

Choosing the right long-term policy is essential for anyone focusing on comprehensive and strategic retirement planning. With the rising costs of medical care and the increasing life expectancy, long-term care (LTC) insurance has become more relevant than ever. But how do you pick the right policy that ensures both your financial stability and your healthcare needs? Let's dig into this, and I'll guide you through some key steps.

First of all, you need to assess your future healthcare needs. Take a moment to reflect on your family's medical history, your current health status, and potential future medical conditions. Understanding the potential risks can help you decide on the type and extent of coverage you'll need. For instance, if there's a history of Alzheimer's or other chronic illnesses in your family, a comprehensive LTC policy might be more suitable.

Secondly, consider your financial situation. Examine your current income, savings, and any other investments. The cost of long-term care can be steep, and LTC insurance premiums can vary significantly. It's critical to choose a policy you can afford now and continue to afford in the future. You don't want to be hit with unexpectedly high premiums in your retirement years, so factor in possible inflation and the increasing costs of healthcare.

The next step is to understand the policy options available in the market. Not all long-term care policies are created equal. Some cover only nursing home care, while others extend to in-home care, adult daycare, or assisted living facilities. You'll need a clear idea of what type of care you envision needing. Look into policies that offer a range of care options, as flexibility can be crucial over time.

Research the insurance providers thoroughly. Financial stability and the company's track record are key indicators of reliability. Look at reviews, ratings from financial organizations, and even customer testimonials. Trustworthy insurers not only provide consistent service but also ensure that claims are handled without undue stress. You want your policy to be dependable when you need it most.

Policy terms and conditions are another critical aspect to scrutinize. The elimination period, also known as the waiting period, can affect your out-of-pocket expenses. This is the amount of time you'll need to pay for care before your policy begins to pay out. Typically, shorter elimination periods mean higher premiums, so you'll need to balance these periods against your financial preparedness.

Coverage limits and benefit periods are also crucial. A policy may offer daily, monthly, or lifetime caps on benefits. You'll have to consider how long you might need care and how much it could cost daily. Policies that offer inflation protection can be particularly beneficial, ensuring that your coverage keeps pace with rising healthcare costs.

Evaluate the services bundled with the policy. Some LTC policies come with additional features such as care coordination services, respite care for family caregivers, or home modification benefits. These added features can provide not just financial support but also practical assistance, reducing the burden on your family.

Personalization is key. A one-size-fits-all approach rarely works with long-term care insurance. Many providers allow customization of policies to better fit individual needs. Customizable options might include choosing specific benefit amounts, adjusting waiting periods, or deciding on the maximum period of coverage.

Before finalizing anything, consult with a financial advisor or insurance expert. Their expertise can provide invaluable insights into policy nuances that you might not fully understand. They'll help you align your LTC policy with your broader retirement strategy, ensuring that everything works seamlessly together.

Don't forget to read the fine print. Clauses regarding pre-existing conditions, policy renewal terms, and situations that might lead to the policy being voided are vital to understand. Ignorance is not bliss when it comes to insurance; knowing every detail ensures you won't be caught off guard when you need to make a claim.

Additionally, keep an eye on state partnership programs. Many states have partnered with insurance companies to offer LTC policies that protect more of your assets if you exhaust your policy benefits and need to rely on Medicaid. These programs can add another layer of security to your financial planning.

Consider the timing of your purchase. Long-term care insurance is typically cheaper the earlier you buy it. Waiting until you're older or experiencing health issues can make premiums prohibitively expensive or might even disqualify you from getting coverage altogether. It's a proactive step that pays off in the long run.

Review your policy periodically. Life circumstances change, and your LTC insurance should adapt accordingly. Regularly revisiting your policy ensures it still aligns with your needs and financial situation. Make adjustments as necessary to maintain adequate coverage.

Ultimately, choosing the right long-term care policy comes down to informed decision-making and being proactive. It's a significant element in constructing a robust retirement plan. With the right LTC insurance policy, you can preserve your financial independence and ensure that you have the care you need when you need it, giving you peace of mind and a more secure future.

Chapter 5:
Health Insurance Options for Retirees

Health insurance is a crucial component of any comprehensive retirement plan, offering peace of mind and protection against unexpected medical costs. As retirees transition into this new phase of life, understanding the various health insurance options becomes paramount. Medicare, with its different parts and supplemental policies, serves as the cornerstone for many, but it's essential to consider alternatives to traditional health insurance as well. Whether it's Medicare Advantage plans, Medigap policies, or private insurance, each option carries its own set of benefits and potential drawbacks. Navigating these choices requires a blend of strategic planning and informed decision-making, ensuring that healthcare needs are met without compromising financial stability. By thoughtfully selecting the right health insurance strategy, retirees can safeguard their health and finances, paving the way for a more secure and enjoyable retirement journey.

Medicare and Supplemental Policies

These are foundational elements for securing your financial stability during retirement. As you transition from employer-provided health insurance to Medicare, understanding the different components and benefits of Medicare is crucial. Medicare alone, however, often falls short in covering all medical expenses. This is where supplemental insurance policies, commonly known as Medigap, come into play, bridging the gap in coverage and ensuring you have comprehensive protection.

Medicare, the federal health insurance program for people aged 65 and over, comes in four parts: Part A, Part B, Part C, and Part D. Part A typically covers hospital stays, skilled nursing facility care, and some home health care. Part B covers outpatient care, preventive services, and some medical equipment. Medicare Part C, or Medicare Advantage, is an alternative to traditional Medicare where private insurers offer bundled plans. Lastly, Part D provides prescription drug coverage, reducing the out-of-pocket costs for medications.

Despite the range of services Medicare provides, there are gaps. For instance, Medicare doesn't cover long-term care, dental, vision, or hearing aids. Co-payments, coinsurances, and deductibles under Part A and Part B can add up quickly, especially with prolonged medical treatments or unexpected emergencies. These gaps necessitate a supplemental policy to maintain financial stability and peace of mind.

Medigap policies come into play here. These are standardized policies offered by private insurers to complement your original Medicare coverage. The key benefits of Medigap policies include covering the costs of coinsurance, co-payments, and deductibles that Medicare Part A and Part B do not cover. This can significantly reduce your out-of-pocket expenses, making healthcare costs more predictable and manageable.

When considering a Medigap policy, it's essential to evaluate your healthcare needs and financial situation. There are ten standardized Medigap plans available, labeled A through N, each offering a different combination of benefits. Plan F, for instance, is considered the most comprehensive, covering almost all out-of-pocket costs. However, since January 1, 2020, Plan F is no longer available to new enrollees, spotlighting the importance of staying updated on policy changes.

To choose the right Medigap plan, start by analyzing your current and anticipated healthcare needs. Ask yourself questions such as: Do I have any chronic conditions requiring frequent doctor visits? Am I on multiple prescription medications? Understanding your specific needs will help you select a plan that provides the most cost-effective coverage.

Remember that selecting a Medigap policy is not a one-time decision. Your needs may evolve, and periodic reviews of your policy, along with any changes in Medicare regulations, are critical. This proactive approach ensures that your coverage remains adequate and cost-efficient throughout your retirement.

Beyond Medigap, another option to consider is Medicare Advantage (Part C) plans. These plans are an alternative to traditional Medicare and often come bundled with Part A, Part B, and Part D coverage. Some Medicare Advantage plans also offer additional benefits such as vision, dental, and wellness programs. The trade-off, however, is that these plans typically require you to use a network of doctors and hospitals.

It's worth noting that Medicare Advantage plans often have lower premiums than Medigap plans, but they might come with higher out-of-pocket expenses. Weighing these factors carefully and comparing plans during the open enrollment period is key to optimizing your healthcare coverage in retirement.

When navigating through the details of Medicare and supplemental policies, it's helpful to utilize tools and resources available through the Medicare website and consultation with insurance agents who specialize in Medicare products. These resources can provide personalized advice and comparative data to help you make informed decisions.

If you're still actively employed and receiving health benefits through your employer, transitioning to Medicare may seem daunting. Understanding the coordination of benefits between your current health insurance and Medicare is imperative. Often, employer health plans become secondary coverage once Medicare kicks in, which could affect your choice and timing of getting a supplemental policy.

Planning for healthcare costs in retirement shouldn't be overwhelming. By being informed and proactive, you can ensure that your medical needs won't impose unexpected financial burdens. Incorporating Medicare and supplemental policies into your retirement plan is a strategic move that promotes long-term financial security and peace of mind.

Investigating other forms of supplemental coverage like Medicare Savings Programs (MSPs) for those with limited income or Special Needs Plans (SNPs) for people with specific diseases or health conditions can also enhance your coverage. These options can offer extra aid in managing healthcare expenses.

Engaging with a financial advisor who understands the nuances of Medicare and supplemental policies can add an extra layer of assurance. An advisor can help you navigate changes in healthcare needs and adjust your insurance plans accordingly, ensuring you maintain appropriate coverage without paying for unnecessary extras.

Your goal is to create a seamless and secure health insurance plan that supports your overall retirement strategy. By strategically incorporating Medicare and supplemental policies, you lay a robust foundation for a financially secure and healthy retirement. Remember, your healthcare needs are as unique as your retirement plans, and there's a policy combination out there tailored to fit them perfectly.

In conclusion, understanding and effectively utilizing Medicare and supplemental policies is pivotal in retirement planning. These tools offer the peace of mind that comes from knowing you're well-covered, allowing you to enjoy your retirement years without the anxiety of unexpected medical expenses. Stay informed, review your coverage regularly, and take the necessary steps to ensure your healthcare strategy supports your broader retirement goals.

Alternatives to Traditional Health Insurance

Alternatives to Traditional Health Insurance are gaining attention, particularly among retirees looking for flexible and cost-effective solutions. With the rising costs of conventional health insurance and the complexities that come with navigating Medicare and supplemental policies, many are exploring other options to fill the gap. Let's dive into some powerful alternatives that can simplify your healthcare planning and offer more control over your finances.

One popular alternative to traditional health insurance is the Health Savings Account (HSA). An HSA is a tax-advantaged account that allows you to save money specifically for medical expenses. Contributions are tax-deductible, the funds grow tax-free, and withdrawals for qualified medical expenses aren't taxed. This triple tax advantage makes HSAs an incredibly attractive option for many retirees. Plus, after age 65, the funds can be used for non-medical expenses without penalty, though they will be subject to income tax.

An HSA is usually paired with a high-deductible health plan (HDHP), which typically has lower premiums than traditional plans. This combination can reduce your monthly expenses and give you more financial freedom. By strategically using an HSA, you can set aside funds during your working years and tap into them when you need healthcare services in retirement.

Healthcare sharing ministries are another burgeoning alternative. These organizations aren't insurance companies, but they do offer a way for members to share medical costs. Members of healthcare sharing ministries contribute monthly dues, which go towards paying for the medical expenses of other members. While these programs often have religious affiliations and may not cover all types of medical care, they can offer a sense of community and support.

One advantage of healthcare sharing ministries is that they can be significantly cheaper than traditional health insurance. However, it's crucial to read the fine print carefully. These programs are not regulated in the same way as insurance products, and they may have limitations that traditional insurance would not. So, always ensure the program aligns with your healthcare needs and values.

Concierge medicine, also known as retainer medicine, is attracting those willing to pay a bit more for direct and personalized healthcare. In this model, you pay an annual or monthly fee for unlimited access to your primary care physician. This fee covers a comprehensive range of services, including extended consultation times and 24/7 access. For retirees looking for a high-touch healthcare experience, concierge medicine can be both reassuring and effective.

Direct Primary Care (DPC) is a similar concept to concierge medicine but often comes at a lower cost. With DPC, you usually pay a flat monthly fee to a primary care doctor who provides a wide range of services in-house. This model eliminates the need for insurance in many instances, cutting down on both costs and administrative burdens. Many DPC practices also negotiate discounts for their patients on lab work, imaging, and prescriptions, making it a comprehensive and often more affordable option.

Another intriguing choice for some retirees is the use of telemedicine services. Telemedicine involves consulting healthcare providers remotely, using video calls or internet-based platforms. These services can be a cost-effective alternative for managing minor ailments and chronic conditions, and they offer the convenience of accessing care from the comfort of your home. Many telemedicine providers offer monthly subscription plans, which can be a valuable addition to your healthcare toolkit.

Short-term health insurance plans can be beneficial for those who need temporary coverage, perhaps while transitioning between traditional plans or waiting for Medicare eligibility. These plans are generally less expensive than comprehensive plans and provide coverage for unexpected illnesses or accidents for a limited period. Be mindful, though; they typically do not cover preexisting conditions and may have other limitations, so they should be used strategically.

Retirees living abroad might find international health insurance plans more suited to their needs. These plans cater specifically to expatriates and often provide more extensive coverage globally than domestic policies. They offer flexibility and can be tailored to include emergency evacuation, which is a critical consideration if you plan to spend significant time overseas. Costs can vary widely, so it's essential to carefully compare options and understand what's covered.

Joining a medical cost-sharing group tailored for specific communities or lifestyles can also be a viable option. These groups often operate on a similar principle to healthcare sharing ministries but are more secular and inclusive. They offer another avenue to share medical expenses with others, thus potentially reducing your healthcare costs.

Hybrid insurance products are another alternative worth exploring. Some life insurance policies and annuities come with riders that offer benefits similar to long-term care insurance or critical illness coverage. These hybrid products can serve dual purposes, providing both death benefits and living benefits to cover significant healthcare costs. They can be particularly appealing for those looking to maximize the utility of their insurance dollar.

Cash indemnity plans, though less common, can also offer a supplementary layer of healthcare coverage. These plans provide a fixed cash benefit for specific medical services or conditions. For example, you might receive a set amount for each day you spend in the hospital. This cash can then be used to cover any out-of-pocket expenses, giving you added financial flexibility.

Lastly, don't overlook the potential of negotiation. Many healthcare providers are open to negotiating the cost of services, particularly if you are paying out-of-pocket. There are also services and apps designed to help you find price transparency and negotiate better rates for medical procedures. Taking a proactive approach can save you significant sums over time.

Exploring these alternatives to traditional health insurance demands a proactive and informed approach. Each option comes with its own set of benefits and trade-offs, making it crucial to align your healthcare strategy with your specific financial and medical needs. As you weigh these alternatives, consider how they fit into your broader retirement planning and financial goals. The ultimate aim is to ensure you have a robust, flexible, and cost-effective healthcare strategy that supports your overall well-being and financial security.

Chapter 6:
Disability Insurance to Protect Your Retirement

When it comes to securing your retirement, many people overlook a key ingredient: disability insurance. This isn't just about safeguarding your income during your working years; it's also a crucial part of protecting your long-term financial health. Imagine if an injury or illness struck tomorrow—how would you continue saving for your golden years? Long-term disability insurance steps in to replace a portion of your income, allowing you to maintain your retirement contributions while covering your daily living expenses. Integrating this insurance with other sources of retirement income, such as Social Security or personal investments, provides a safety net that ensures you don't deplete your retirement savings prematurely. The peace of mind that comes from knowing you're covered can't be overstated. It's time to think beyond immediate needs and consider how disability insurance can play a strategic role in your comprehensive retirement plan, securing a future where financial stability aligns seamlessly with health and well-being.

Long-Term Disability Insurance Explained

Consideration for Long-Term Disability Insurance is critical when planning for a secure retirement. You might be asking why this type of insurance is essential for your retirement strategy in the first place. Imagine you're still a few years away from retiring when an unexpected illness or accident drastically alters your ability to work. Long-term disability insurance (LTD) becomes a financial lifeline, providing income when you can't earn a paycheck. That's precisely why it's worth a closer look.

Long-term disability insurance is designed to replace a portion of your income if you become unable to work for an extended period due to illness or injury. Typically, this insurance kicks in after a waiting period, often referred to as an elimination period, which can range from a few weeks to several months. Depending on the specifics of your policy, benefits will cover up to 60-80% of your monthly income. This ensures that even with a disrupted earning capability, you can still take care of your financial obligations.

Here's a vital aspect to consider: the likelihood of experiencing a disability might be higher than you think. Statistics suggest that more than one in four people entering the workforce today will encounter a disability before they retire. By understanding the risks and proactively securing an LTD policy, you'll protect your retirement savings from being depleted prematurely due to unforeseen circumstances.

Another important feature of long-term disability insurance is that it often covers a broad array of conditions, from chronic illnesses to severe physical injuries. It becomes your financial safety net, ensuring continuity of income. This is crucial for maintaining your standard of living and continuing with your retirement savings plan despite the curveballs life throws at you.

Why is LTD particularly significant for those planning their retirement? For starters, your peak earning years often coincide with the years when you're aggressively saving for retirement. If you suddenly lose the ability to work, not only could you lose out on current income, but you might also miss the chance to make essential contributions to your retirement nest egg. LTD insurance helps bridge this gap, providing the financial stability you need to keep your long-term plans on track.

Moreover, long-term disability benefits are typically paid out until you can return to work or reach the retirement age specified in your policy. This means you won't have to deplete your retirement funds prematurely. When selecting a policy, it's essential to examine the benefit period to ensure it aligns with your anticipated retirement timeline.

Integrating LTD insurance with your overall retirement plan requires a thoughtful approach. Consider working with a financial planner to evaluate how an LTD policy fits within your broader financial strategy. Your planner can help you understand the nuances of LTD policies, such as non-cancellable policies, which guarantee that your premiums and benefits will not change as long as you continue to pay premiums on time.

An often-overlooked factor is the elimination period—the time before benefits kick in after you become disabled. Opting for a longer elimination period usually lowers your premiums but requires having an emergency fund that can cover your expenses during that waiting time. Balancing the elimination period with premium costs is crucial for securing affordable yet comprehensive coverage.

Furthermore, some employers offer group disability insurance as part of their benefits package. While this can be a cost-effective option, such policies often provide limited coverage. Supplementing group insurance with an individual LTD policy ensures you have adequate protection tailored to your income and lifestyle requirements. It's also worth noting whether your employer-provided policy is portable—meaning you can take it with you if you change jobs.

Tax implications are another critical area to keep in mind. Generally, if you pay the premiums with after-tax dollars, the benefits you receive are tax-free. However, if your employer pays the premiums, the benefits may be taxable. Consulting a tax advisor to understand these nuances can help you make a more informed decision and plan for any potential tax liabilities.

A holistic approach to LTD insurance also involves understanding the definitions within your policy. Terms like "own occupation" vs. "any occupation" can significantly impact your benefits. "Own occupation" means you receive benefits if you can't perform the duties of your specific job, whereas "any occupation" implies benefits are only payable if you can't work in any job suited to your education and experience. The clarity in these definitions will help you select the policy that best meets your needs.

Lastly, it's vital to review your LTD insurance periodically. Life circumstances change, and what was sufficient coverage a decade ago might not meet your current needs. Regular updates ensure your policy adapts to your evolving financial and health conditions, providing you with continual security as you approach retirement.

In summary, long-term disability insurance is more than just a protective measure against lost income due to illness or injury; it is a cornerstone of a robust retirement plan. By providing financial stability, it allows you to preserve your retirement savings and continue working toward your long-term financial goals. As you move forward, understanding your needs and the available options will empower you to make informed, strategic decisions that secure your financial future.

Integrating Disability Insurance with Other Retirement Income Sources

Planning for retirement isn't just about securing your golden years; it's about weaving a safety net for life's unforeseen challenges. Disability insurance is a critical, yet often overlooked, cornerstone in this intricate web of financial security. When integrated seamlessly with other retirement income streams, it ensures that unexpected health issues don't derail your financial plans.

Imagine you're set with a well-thought-out retirement plan that includes Social Security, pensions, and personal savings. Suddenly, a disability strikes. How do you maintain your lifestyle? This is where disability insurance steps in, acting as a bridge that connects gaps in your income streams caused by a sudden loss in earning capacity.

First, let's clarify what disability insurance entails. Essentially, it provides income replacement if you're unable to work due to a disabling condition. But to leverage disability insurance effectively, you need to understand how it intertwines with other components of your retirement income. We're talking about a holistic approach where each element—like Social Security benefits, pensions, annuities, and personal savings—plays its part harmoniously.

It's crucial to start with Social Security Disability Insurance (SSDI), which is often the first recourse for those who become disabled before retirement. While SSDI offers support, it might not fully cover all your financial needs. Here's where private disability insurance steps up, filling the financial gaps left by SSDI. Private disability insurance can provide supplemental income to bridge this shortfall.

Balancing these sources begins with understanding the coordination of benefits. If you're already receiving SSDI, private disability insurance typically adjusts its payments to ensure you don't exceed a specified percentage of your pre-disability income. This prevents a redundancy of benefits and ensures you receive a balanced financial support system.

For those fortunate enough to have a pension, the integration of disability insurance becomes even more nuanced. Some pension plans include disability benefits, which might reduce or eliminate the need for a separate disability insurance policy. However, not all pensions are created equal. Evaluate your specific plan to determine if additional disability coverage is necessary.

Personal savings and investments are pivotal components of your retirement portfolio that need safeguarding. The loss of income due to a disability can force you to tap into these savings earlier than planned. Disability insurance helps preserve these assets by providing ongoing income, preventing premature withdrawals that can deplete your retirement nest egg.

Annuities serve as another vital pillar that can be coordinated with disability insurance. If you've invested in an immediate or deferred annuity, consider how disability insurance payouts will interact with these streams. In many cases, the steady income from an annuity can complement disability benefits, providing financial stability while ensuring that long-term goals remain intact.

Let's not overlook the tax implications of integrating these income sources. Typically, SSDI benefits might be taxable if your overall income surpasses certain thresholds. Conversely, the payouts from private disability insurance are generally tax-free if you paid the premiums with after-tax dollars. Understanding these nuances helps in effectively planning your cash flow and tax liabilities.

Besides financial considerations, think about the peace of mind and emotional security offered by a well-integrated plan. A sudden disability can be emotionally draining, and the last thing you want is financial stress adding to the burden. Having a coordinated strategy ensures you can focus on your recovery and well-being, knowing your finances are under control.

Effective integration also involves regular reviews of your policies and financial status. Life circumstances change, and so should your planning strategies. Regularly updating your disability insurance policies and retirement plans ensures they remain aligned with your current needs and future goals.

Communication with your financial advisor is another key element. Keep them in the loop about any changes in your health, income, or retirement plans. They can provide invaluable guidance on how to adapt your strategy effectively, ensuring that all pieces of your financial puzzle fit together seamlessly.

Ultimately, the goal is to create a robust, multi-layered safety net. By strategically integrating disability insurance with other retirement income sources, you create a comprehensive financial framework. This ensures that life's uncertainties don't jeopardize the retirement you've worked so hard to build.

Embarking on this planning journey requires both foresight and flexibility. It's about anticipating the unexpected and having the right measures in place to tackle any curveballs that come your way. When you think about retirement, don't just think about relaxation—think about resilience. Because a resilient retirement plan isn't just about enjoying the fruits of your labor; it's about being prepared for whatever life throws at you.

By melding your disability insurance with other income sources, you're not just piecing together a retirement plan; you're crafting a comprehensive life strategy that ensures security, dignity, and peace of mind, no matter what challenges lie ahead.

Chapter 7:
Liability Insurance in Retirement

As you navigate the complexities of retirement planning, liability insurance stands out as a crucial yet often overlooked element for ensuring comprehensive financial security. In your golden years, you might assume that the risks associated with legal liability reduce, but the reality is quite different. Accidents can still happen, and the financial repercussions can be severe if you're not adequately protected. An umbrella insurance policy offers extensive coverage beyond the limits of your existing homeowners and auto policies, safeguarding your assets from significant legal claims. Assessing your liability risks involves considering not only your current lifestyle but also potential future scenarios such as injuries on your property or even claims related to volunteer activities. Knowing how to protect yourself with the right liability insurance can ensure your peace of mind, letting you focus on enjoying retirement without the looming threat of unforeseen legal expenses. So, dive deeper into understanding the scope and benefits of these policies to make informed decisions that bolster your retirement plan.

Umbrella Policies for Comprehensive Protection

This option provides an essential safety net, extending beyond standard insurance policies to cover unforeseen gaps. It's more than just an additional layer—it's a bolstering of your financial fortress, ensuring you're shielded against life's unpredictable nature. But why should retirees, in particular, prioritize an umbrella policy? Let's break it down.

First off, it's crucial to recognize that as you age, your asset base typically expands. Your home, investments, savings, and even your cherished collections hold considerable value. An umbrella policy extends liability coverage beyond the limits of your homeowners, auto, and other personal insurance policies. This additional coverage can be vital when the unexpected happens—like an accident on your property or a major car collision—events that could potentially exceed the limits of your basic policies.

Moreover, retirees often have mixed-use properties and hobbies that might bring additional risk. Think about renting out a vacation home or enjoying a recreational vehicle. These activities, while enriching and enjoyable, introduce complexities and liabilities. Umbrella insurance can cover lawsuits related to these additional risks, offering peace of mind that you won't have to liquidate assets or tap into retirement funds to cover legal fees or settlements.

One of the most compelling reasons to consider an umbrella policy during retirement is its cost-effectiveness. Compared to the significant coverage it provides—often in the range of $1 million to $5 million— umbrella insurance is relatively inexpensive. This makes it one of the most efficient ways to protect your retirement nest egg from substantial claims and litigation that might not be covered by standard liability limits.

What's oftentimes overlooked is that an umbrella policy isn't just about protecting assets; it's about securing your lifestyle. Your retirement years should be spent enjoying your hard-earned freedom, not worrying about potential financial ruin from legal battles. Umbrella insurance helps to ensure that you can maintain your standard of living and continue with your planned activities without undue concern about extensive financial exposure.

Additionally, umbrella policies can cover a range of incidents and lawsuits that aren't typically covered by regular insurance policies. For example, it might include protection against claims of slander, libel, or defamation of character—risks that, while uncommon, can have substantial repercussions, particularly in an increasingly digital age where a casual comment online can lead to serious litigation.

Given the evolving landscape of risk management, umbrella insurance also integrates seamlessly with other insurance strategies. When planning your comprehensive retirement strategy, you can align your umbrella policy with other protections like long-term care insurance, health insurance, and estate planning tools. This holistic approach optimizes your overall safety net, ensuring that all aspects of potential risk are mitigated.

As you evaluate your need for an umbrella policy, an essential step is to assess your current liability limits. Take a close look at your homeowner's and auto insurance policies. How much coverage do they provide, and are these amounts enough to cover your total assets? If the answer is no, an umbrella policy becomes more than just advisable—it becomes crucial.

Consulting with a financial advisor can offer personalized insights into how an umbrella policy can fit into your existing insurance portfolio. They can guide you on how much coverage is appropriate based on your unique financial situation, lifestyle, and risk exposure. Their expertise ensures that your coverage is both adequate and cost-effective, aligning perfectly with your broader retirement goals.

Understanding the exact scenarios that an umbrella policy covers is also vital. These policies often have exceptions and exclusions. Make sure you read the fine print to understand what's included and what isn't. This way, you won't be caught off guard in the unlikely event that a claim falls outside of your coverage parameters.

Another key consideration is the inclusion of uninsured and underinsured motorist coverage, which can be a valuable addition to an umbrella policy. This can provide substantial protection in cases where you're involved in an accident with someone who doesn't have sufficient insurance, another common retirement risk given the increased travel often enjoyed in retirement.

When integrated with estate planning, umbrella policies offer an additional safeguard for your heirs. This ensures that their inheritance isn't compromised by unforeseen lawsuits or claims against your estate. It gives you the confidence that your legacy will remain intact, allowing your beneficiaries to inherit as you intended.

Moreover, umbrella insurance encourages retirees to think beyond the immediate and obvious. Yes, it covers additional financial liabilities, but it might also push you to review and improve safety measures within your home, driving habits, and overall lifestyle to mitigate risks further.

In sum, an umbrella policy is not just an additional insurance product—it's a strategic component of a comprehensive retirement plan. It allows you to enjoy your well-deserved retirement with confidence, knowing that you've fortified your financial defenses against unknown threats. It embodies the principle of hope for the best, but prepare for the worst, ensuring that your golden years remain golden through any storm you might face.

Assessing Your Liability Risks

Assessing Your Liability Risks is a crucial step toward ensuring your retirement remains secure and free from unexpected financial pitfalls. Liability risks, by their very nature, are unpredictable and often underestimated. Taking the time to thoroughly evaluate these risks can provide peace of mind and a sturdier financial foundation as you enter your golden years.

Let's start by understanding what liability risks actually encompass. Liability risks are those that pertain to your legal responsibility for any harm or damage you might cause inadvertently to others. This could stem from several scenarios, including accidents on your property, automobile incidents, or even personal actions that result in legal consequences. The financial impact of these events can be devastating without proper preparation and coverage.

First, consider your lifestyle and daily activities. Are you hosting gatherings at your home? Do you frequently travel? Do you own valuable items that could potentially cause damage if mishandled? Each of these activities can increase your liability risk. By identifying the activities that most significantly expose you to risk, you can better understand how to mitigate them.

Owning property is one of the primary sources of liability risk. Whether it's your residence or an additional property, there are inherent dangers—slip, trips, and falls being the most common. Ensuring your home is safe and addressing any potential hazards can substantially reduce your liability. Additionally, reviewing your homeowners' insurance policy to confirm it provides adequate coverage in the event of an accident is essential.

Automobile ownership is another significant area to examine. Car accidents can lead to costly medical bills, repairs, and even legal fees if you're found at fault. Make sure your auto insurance policy offers sufficient liability coverage to protect against these expenses. Some policies may only cover a minimal amount, which may not be enough depending on the severity of the accident.

Next, think about any hobbies that might carry liability risks. If you're a boating enthusiast, for instance, you have to account for the potential accidents that could occur on the water. Similarly, owning pets, particularly dogs, can bring additional concerns if your pet were to bite or injure someone. Exploring specialized insurance coverage tailored to these activities can safeguard your finances and provide a buffer against unexpected incidents.

Now, consider your online presence and activities. In today's digital age, the internet can also pose liability risks. Cyber liabilities, such as inadvertently posting sensitive information or falling prey to identity theft, can have serious financial implications. Look into personal liability insurance that covers cyber threats to shield yourself from these modern-day hazards.

Umbrella policies are a powerful tool for mitigating liability risks. These policies provide an additional layer of protection on top of your existing insurance coverage, filling in the gaps where traditional policies might fall short. For example, if a claim exceeds the limits of your homeowners or auto insurance, an umbrella policy can cover the remaining costs, preventing a financial disaster.

When assessing your liability risks, it's also important to consider potential future changes. Are you planning any renovations? As your circumstances evolve, so too should your insurance coverage to ensure it continues to meet your needs. Regularly reviewing and updating your policies in consultation with a knowledgeable insurance advisor can help manage these transitions smoothly.

One should not overlook the importance of legal consultation when evaluating liability risks. An experienced attorney can offer valuable insights into potential legal pitfalls and advise you on structuring your assets to minimize exposure. Legal fees might seem like an added expense, but they pale in comparison to the costs associated with a significant liability claim.

Another key component is documenting and maintaining thorough records. Whether it's proof of home safety measures, maintenance logs for your car, or receipts for any valuables you own, having detailed documentation can simplify the claims process and support your case if a liability issue arises.

Assessing your liability risks is also about understanding the interconnectedness of various insurance products. For instance, how does your health insurance play into your liability risk management? In the case of a personal injury claim, does your health insurance cover some of the costs? Evaluating these interdependencies can uncover gaps and highlight areas where additional coverage might be necessary.

Think about how you interact with your community. If you're involved in volunteer work or serve on a board, these activities could heighten your liability exposure. Specific insurance coverage, such as directors and officers liability insurance, might be relevant in these scenarios. A comprehensive approach considers all facets of your life that could pose a risk.

Lastly, don't neglect to educate those around you about liability risks. Family members, especially those living in your household, should be aware of potential hazards and how to avoid them. Shared understanding and proactive measures can create a safer environment and minimize the likelihood of liability incidents occurring in the first place.

In sum, by methodically assessing and addressing your liability risks, you fortify your retirement plan against unforeseen financial setbacks. It's about being proactive, informed, and mindful of the details that others might overlook. Taking the time to thoroughly evaluate these aspects today can save you from significant hardship and ensure your financial stability and peace of mind in the future.

Chapter 8:
Property and Casualty
Insurance for Retirees

As you transition into retirement, securing your tangible assets becomes paramount. Property and casualty insurance, covering areas such as homeowners, auto, and additional properties, provides essential safeguards for your retirement years. The dynamic nature of these insurance products means they can be tailored to suit changing retirement needs, allowing for both protection and peace of mind. It's important to periodically review and adjust your policies to align with your evolving lifestyle. Retirees should consider factors like potential changes in living arrangements and vehicle usage, ensuring they remain adequately covered without overpaying. By integrating these insurance strategies effectively, you're not just protecting assets — you're enhancing your overall financial security, ready to face any unexpected events with confidence.

Homeowners and Auto Insurance Considerations

These insurances are often overlooked when planning for retirement, but they play a crucial role in ensuring your financial security. As you transition into retirement, your needs and circumstances change, and so should your insurance policies. Let's start by looking at the primary reasons why keeping your homeowners and auto insurance up-to-date is essential.

First, your home is likely one of your most valuable assets. As such, protecting it should be a top priority. When you retire, you might find yourself spending more time at home, increasing the necessity for comprehensive homeowners insurance. This policy not only covers the physical structure but also protects your personal belongings and provides liability coverage in case someone is injured on your property.

A significant consideration for retirees is ensuring your homeowners insurance covers the replacement cost of your home. This is the amount it would cost to rebuild your home from scratch, including materials and labor, which can be affected by inflation and rising construction costs. An up-to-date policy will help ensure you're covered for these eventualities.

Next, let's talk about personal property coverage. As retirees, you may have accumulated valuable items over the years—jewelry, art, collectibles—that might not be fully covered under a standard homeowners policy. You should consider adding a personal property floater or endorsement to your policy to provide additional protection for these valuable items.

Liability coverage in homeowners insurance is another crucial aspect. This part of your policy protects you if someone gets injured on your property and decides to sue. As you may host more family gatherings or community events in retirement, the risk of accidents happening on your property rises. Ensuring you have adequate liability coverage can help protect your retirement savings from potential lawsuits.

Turning to auto insurance, it's essential to re-evaluate your coverage as you age. With retirement often comes a reduction in daily commuting and overall driving. This means you might be eligible for lower premiums. Contact your insurance provider to see if you can benefit from such reductions if you're driving less.

Despite driving less, the importance of carrying sufficient auto insurance cannot be overstated. Medical costs and vehicle repair expenses can quickly deplete retirement savings if you're underinsured. Make sure your auto policy includes ample liability coverage, which protects you financially if you're found responsible for an accident involving injury or property damage.

Another consideration is whether you'll be using your car for travel during retirement. Extended road trips may require you to rethink your coverage. Breakdown coverages or rental car reimbursement policies can offer peace of mind should you encounter mechanical issues or accidents far from home.

Now, let's discuss technological advancements in automobiles. Many modern cars come equipped with various safety features such as automatic emergency braking and lane departure warnings. These features can sometimes qualify you for discounts on your auto insurance. Be sure to inform your insurer of any such additions.

For those planning to downsize or relocate in retirement, understanding the implications for your homeowners and auto insurance is critical. Moving to a different geographic area can affect your premiums due to the varying risks associated with different locations—think natural disasters, crime rates, etc. Make sure to reassess your coverage needs in light of these changes.

Bundling your homeowners and auto insurance policies can provide significant savings. Insurers often offer discounts when you hold multiple policies with them. This can be a cost-effective way to maintain comprehensive coverage without breaking the bank.

While focusing on financial savings, don't forget to review your deductible amounts. A higher deductible can lower your premiums, but it means you'll pay more out-of-pocket in the event of a claim.

Given the importance of preserving your retirement funds, balance your deductible to optimize both coverage and out-of-pocket costs.

As part of your retirement planning, regularly review and update your insurance policies. Life changes, property upgrades, or even alterations in your driving patterns necessitate adjustments in your coverage. Periodic reviews ensure that you remain adequately protected without overpaying for unnecessary coverage.

Remember, the purpose of homeowners and auto insurance is to safeguard your lifestyle and finances against unforeseen events. As such, these considerations are an integral part of a comprehensive retirement strategy. By staying proactive and informed, you can enjoy your retirement years with peace of mind, knowing you have the necessary protections in place.

Insurance for Other Assets and Properties

Insurance for Other Assets and Properties encompasses a crucial aspect of solidifying your retirement plans. It's not just about protecting your home or car; imagine all the other valuable assets you own: boats, art collections, rental properties, or even a small business. Each of these significant investments deserves comprehensive insurance coverage to safeguard your financial future.

The thought of insuring other assets might initially seem overwhelming. Where does one begin? First, take inventory of all your valuable assets. You can't insure what you don't know you have. For high-value belongings such as jewelry or art, specific policies like personal articles floaters could be your best bet. These policies often provide broader coverage than standard homeowner's insurance.

Another pivotal area is vacation homes or rental properties. An additional property might be a lucrative investment and a slice of your retirement dream. However, these properties come with their own set of risks—tenants, maintenance issues, and natural disasters, to name a few. Specialized landlord insurance can often cover lost rental income, property damage, and even liability protection in case someone gets injured on your premises.

When insuring recreational vehicles like boats or RVs, you might wonder how they fit into a retirement strategy. Well, they represent more than leisure—they signify mobility and quality of life. Marine insurance or motorhome coverage ensures that these investments don't sink your plans due to unforeseen mishaps. You worked hard for these aspects of your lifestyle; don't leave them unprotected.

Personal liability also extends to a broader spectrum when you own diverse assets. Umbrella policies offer an extra layer of security. If a claim exceeds the limits of your standard policies, umbrella insurance steps in to cover the gap, giving you peace of mind that your retirement savings remain intact. This is about securing more than just immediate loss; it's about holistic financial protection.

High-net-worth individuals might find standard insurance policies insufficient for sizeable estates or rare items. This is where custom insurance products tailored for valuable collections, like antiques, wines, or even classic cars, come into play. These policies generally offer higher coverage limits and a deeper understanding of the unique risks associated with such assets.

Don't overlook smaller, yet significant, assets like musical instruments or expensive electronics. With the rise of remote work and hobbies in retirement, gadgets and equipment become essential. Ensuring they are covered under a policy that accounts for their replacement value can save future headaches. In many cases, you can add these items to your existing homeowner's policy as scheduled personal property.

While there's surely a lot to consider, navigating through specialized insurance products for other assets doesn't have to be a solo journey. Working closely with an insurance agent familiar with retirement planning can provide valuable insights. They can help tailor policies to fit your unique portfolio of assets, making sure you're covered comprehensively and efficiently.

Business owners transitioning into retirement face the additional challenge of securing their business assets. Business insurance, including liability, property, and business interruption insurance, is essential. This coverage not only protects the business but also safeguards your personal finances tied to it. Selling the business? Transactional insurance can help manage the risks involved in the process, protecting both buyer and seller.

The digital age brings another consideration. What about digital assets—photos, documents, or cryptocurrencies? While insuring digital assets is a relatively new concept, some insurance companies offer policies extending to data breaches and digital loss, particularly beneficial for those heavily reliant on technology. Similarly, cybersecurity insurance could be considered if you manage substantial online transactions or sensitive personal data.

One often neglected but crucial area is liability related to pets. Yes, your furry companion can also create financial liability, especially if they cause harm or damage. Some homeowner's policies can extend to cover such incidents, but dedicated pet liability insurance might be more appropriate, depending on your circumstances.

Unearthing the right insurance mix to cover all additional assets involves a proactive approach. Regular assessments and adjustments of your coverage ensure it continues to align with your assets' current value and your retirement aspirations. Don't set it and forget it; life's changes demand that your insurance strategy evolves as well.

At its core, the idea isn't just about insuring material possessions but securing peace of mind. Robust insurance for other assets glues together various aspects of your retirement plan, ensuring that any unexpected property issue doesn't dismantle your financial stability.

With the piecemeal protection of your diversified assets, the drive is simple: steer clear of losses draining your well-earned nest egg. As you curate your retirement blueprint, interspersing it with meticulous insurance details, you're building a fortified path to an untroubled future.

In conclusion, "Insurance for Other Assets and Properties" involves a comprehensive look at all your valuable belongings and investments beyond the typical scope. Addressing each with tailored insurance ensures that no stone is left unturned in your pursuit of a secure, well-rounded retirement. It's about living your golden years without the ever-looming worry of the 'what ifs'. By fortifying your array of assets with the appropriate insurance products, you're not just protecting items but, fundamentally, safeguarding your way of life.

Chapter 9:
The Role of Social Security in Retirement Planning

As we traverse the road of retirement planning, understanding the role of Social Security in your financial strategy is paramount. Social Security benefits are often a bedrock for many retirees, providing a dependable income stream that can ease the strain on personal savings. The foundational aspect of these benefits isn't just about knowing when to claim; it's about integrating them with your broader financial and insurance plans to maximize their impact. This chapter will guide you through aligning Social Security benefits with other sources of retirement income, ensuring a balanced approach that addresses both present needs and long-term stability. With the right approach, Social Security can do more than just supplement your income—it can act as a catalyst for achieving a secure and fulfilling retirement, blending seamlessly with the other insurance components discussed in previous chapters. Let's unlock the potential of Social Security in creating a resilient retirement strategy tailored just for you.

Maximizing Social Security Benefits

Maximizing Social Security Benefits is crucial for building a robust retirement plan and ensuring long-term financial stability. For many, Social Security forms a backbone of retirement income, making its optimization one of the smartest moves you can make. But, the details can get complicated. Let's unpack the nuances to help you get the most out of your benefits.

First off, timing is everything when it comes to Social Security. You can start claiming benefits as early as age 62, but there's a trade-off. Early claims lead to permanently reduced monthly payments. On the other hand, delaying benefits past your full retirement age (usually between 66 and 67, depending on your birth year) can boost your payments by up to 8% per year until you turn 70. Those extra sums can add up significantly, offering you greater financial flexibility in your later years.

The concept of "break-even age" is essential here. This is the point in time when the total benefits received from delaying outweigh those from taking them early. Calculating this correctly can guide you on whether to start early or wait. While you can't predict the future, considering factors like your health, life expectancy, and financial situation helps in making an informed decision.

Next, let's address the impact of spousal benefits. If you're married, recognizing the interplay between your benefits and your spouse's benefits can give you additional leverage. Generally, you're entitled to receive up to 50% of your spouse's benefit amount if that is higher than your own. But decisions here aren't clear-cut and depend heavily on each spouse's work history and age.

In cases where one spouse has significantly higher earnings, a "file and suspend" strategy can be beneficial. This involves one spouse filing for benefits at full retirement age and then immediately suspending them. This way, the other spouse can claim spousal benefits while the primary earner allows their own benefits to grow until age 70. However, note that changes in Social Security regulations sometimes limit such strategies, so always check current rules.

Widow and widower benefits add another layer of complexity. If one spouse passes away, the surviving spouse can claim the deceased's benefits if they're higher than their own. Timing plays a crucial role here too. You don't necessarily need to claim them immediately, especially if delaying can bring you those higher payments later on.

And let's not forget about divorced spouse benefits. If you've been married for at least ten years and are currently unmarried, you might be eligible for benefits based on your ex-spouse's work record. This often-overlooked route gives opportunities for additional income streams that could significantly ease financial burdens during retirement.

Moreover, working while collecting Social Security can affect your benefits if you haven't reached full retirement age yet. Earnings above specific thresholds result in temporary benefit reductions. Once you hit full retirement age, however, those withheld benefits are recalculated and added back in over time, ensuring you're not ultimately short-changed.

Another pivotal aspect is taxation of Social Security benefits. Depending on your combined income, up to 85% of your benefits may be taxable. Knowing this, you can structure other income sources, like withdrawals from Roth IRAs or certain life insurance products, to minimize your taxable income and thus optimize your net benefit.

Coordinating Social Security with your broader retirement portfolio is equally vital. Social Security alone likely won't cover all your needs, but it provides a reliable, inflation-adjusted base. Integrating it with annuities, pensions, and other investments can craft a comprehensive and resilient retirement plan. The goal is to create multiple streams of income, reducing overall risk and enhancing financial security.

Consider also the role of healthcare expenses in your Social Security strategy. Given rising medical costs, part of your benefits might need to cover Medicare premiums and other out-of-pocket health expenses. Supplementing Social Security with long-term care insurance can help safeguard your finances from unexpected medical events.

Lastly, understanding legislative changes is pivotal. Social Security isn't immune to policy shifts. Regularly reviewing updates and adapting your strategy accordingly ensures that you maximize your benefits under the current laws. Engaging with a financial advisor specializing in retirement planning can provide customized advice and keep you informed on legislative trends.

In conclusion, maximizing Social Security benefits requires a detailed, strategic approach. By carefully considering timing, spousal benefits, work implications, taxation, and integration with other income sources, you set yourself up for a financially secure and enjoyable retirement. The effort you put into understanding and optimizing your Social Security can pay significant dividends in your golden years.

Coordinating Social Security with Other Retirement Income

This isn't just a topic—it's a strategic maneuver to secure a financially stable future. One of the most significant challenges retirees face is effectively integrating Social Security with other sources of retirement income. This section will delve into practical ways to balance these streams to maximize your benefits and guarantee lifelong financial peace.

Firstly, let's talk about the timing of your Social Security benefits. Deciding when to start taking Social Security is crucial. The age at which you choose to claim can dramatically affect the amount you receive. You can claim as early as 62, but doing so will reduce your monthly benefit. On the other hand, waiting until full retirement age (FRA) or even later can increase your monthly payout. Your FRA depends on your birth year, but generally falls between 66 and 67.

The decision to delay claiming Social Security might seem like a gamble, but it is often beneficial if you have other sources of income to support you in the meantime. Delaying benefits can increase your monthly payments by approximately 8% per year beyond your FRA, up until age 70. This strategy is often advantageous for those with longer life expectancies or those who have sufficient funds from other sources like pensions, annuities, or retirement savings.

Now, let's look into how to integrate these various income streams. For example, if you have a steady pension, you might not need to tap into Social Security right away. Using your pension while delaying Social Security can boost your future Social Security payments. Also, if you have a significant amount in retirement accounts like a 401(k) or IRA, careful planning around withdrawals can help you maximize benefits.

On the topic of IRAs and 401(k)s, remember that Required Minimum Distributions (RMDs) start at age 72, compelling you to withdraw a certain amount each year. Coordinating your RMDs with your Social Security benefits is another crucial strategy. For instance, withdrawing from your retirement accounts before you start RMDs can preserve your Social Security benefits for later. This is especially useful if you're in a lower tax bracket in the years leading up to mandatory withdrawals.

Annuities also play a significant role in retirement planning. They offer guaranteed income for life and can act as a bridge if you decide to delay Social Security benefits. Some annuities start paying out immediately, while others might be deferred, giving you control over when you receive the income and how it fits into your overall retirement strategy.

When coordinating Social Security with other retirement income, it's also essential to consider taxes. Social Security benefits can be taxable depending on your combined income, which includes wages, self-employment income, interest, dividends, and other taxable income. Integrating tax planning into your strategy can help mitigate the tax burden and optimize your retirement income.

Speaking of taxes, Roth IRAs can be invaluable. Since withdrawals from Roth IRAs are tax-free, they do not contribute to your combined income. This can help keep your Social Security benefits below the taxable threshold. Strategically converting a traditional IRA to a Roth IRA before retirement can offer considerable tax advantages.

Another critical aspect is healthcare and medical expenses, which are bound to rise as you age. Long-term care insurance and health insurance should be factored into your planning. If you spend down your assets for medical expenses, Social Security becomes one of the more predictable sources of income.

Estate planning also ties into this coordination. The aim is to create a financial legacy while factoring in Social Security benefits. Life insurance can cover estate taxes or provide additional funds to descendants, allowing your Social Security benefits to be used for your living expenses.

Moreover, consider survivor benefits. If you are married, delaying Social Security benefits might also increase the survivor benefits for your spouse. Coordinating both spouses' benefits to maximize the payout over your lifetimes can make a considerable difference in ensuring long-term financial security.

Financial advisors often employ software tools to simulate different scenarios and recommend optimal strategies for coordinating

Social Security with other income sources. Using these specialized tools can help fine-tune your retirement plan, ensuring you make the most out of all available resources.

In conclusion, coordinating Social Security with other retirement income sources is a dynamic process that requires careful planning and regular review. Stay informed and proactive. Regularly updating your strategy as circumstances change will help ensure you make the most out of your Social Security benefits and other retirement income streams.

Ultimately, the goal is to create a harmonious balance where your various income streams work together seamlessly to provide a secure, stable, and fulfilling retirement. Whether you're leaning on pensions, annuities, IRAs, or other investments, integrating these with your Social Security benefits correctly will help pave the way for financial security in your golden years.

Chapter 10:
Investment Strategies Integrated with Insurance

In today's complex financial landscape, combining investment strategies with insurance products can be a game-changer for those seeking a secure and prosperous retirement. It's not merely about generating returns; it's about creating a safety net that can weather market volatility and unexpected life events. By integrating insurance with your investment portfolio, you can strike an optimal balance between risk and security, providing stability and potential growth simultaneously. For instance, insurance-backed annuities offer guaranteed income streams, while permanent life insurance policies can serve as both an investment vehicle and a protective shield for your beneficiaries. Diversifying your assets through insurance products not only spreads out risk but also fortifies your financial strategy against unforeseen circumstances. This holistic approach transforms conventional retirement planning into a resilient and adaptive system, ensuring that your golden years are marked by financial freedom and peace of mind. Embracing these integrated strategies equips you with the tools to build a robust financial future, one that's safeguarded by thoughtful, comprehensive planning.

Balancing Risk with Insurance-Backed Investments

This lies at the heart of strategic retirement planning. When considering how to manage the volatility of financial markets while securing steady income streams, insurance-backed investments offer an effective way to mitigate risk. Unlike traditional investments, which can be susceptible to market fluctuations, insurance products add a layer of protection, offering a unique blend of growth potential and security.

So, how exactly do insurance-backed investments help you balance risk? It all boils down to three main factors: capital preservation, steady income streams, and downside protection. Let's dive deeper into these to understand their impact on your retirement portfolio.

Firstly, *capital preservation* is paramount for anyone approaching or already in retirement. At this stage in life, safeguarding your nest egg is crucial. Insurance products such as annuities and indexed universal life insurance (IUL) provide a way to grow your assets while ensuring the principal remains intact. Unlike stocks or mutual funds, which can rapidly depreciate in value, these insurance-backed investments offer guaranteed returns or at least, protection from loss.

Next, we have *steady income streams*. Annuities, for instance, are designed to convert your lump-sum investment into a reliable income stream that can last a lifetime. This is incredibly advantageous when life's unpredictability can at times disrupt financial plans. Annuities ensure you continue to receive income regardless of how long you live, minimizing the risk of outliving your assets.

As for *downside protection*, certain insurance products are structured to shield investors from market downturns. Indexed annuities and IUL policies, for example, offer the potential for growth linked to market indices but with caps and floors. This means you can benefit from market upswings up to a certain limit while being protected from losses during downturns. Essentially, you've got growth potential without the heart-stopping declines that come with market volatility.

Now, let's consider practical implementation. Think of a scenario where you allocate a portion of your retirement savings to an annuity. This decision provides you with a predictable income stream, reducing the amount of income you need to draw from more volatile investments like stocks or bonds. By doing so, you achieve a balanced approach, mitigating risks while allowing room for potential growth. This layered strategy can build a more resilient retirement portfolio.

Moreover, insurance-backed investments bring the benefit of *tax deferral*. Many annuities allow your investment to grow tax-free until you start withdrawing funds. This feature not only boosts the potential for growth but also offers flexibility in tax planning. Instead of facing immediate tax burdens, you can strategically plan withdrawals to efficiently manage your tax liabilities.

Of course, balancing risk doesn't imply insulation from all financial threats. There are fees, surrender charges, and terms that could impact your returns. It's essential to assess the fine print of insurance products and align them with your overall retirement goals. Consulting a financial advisor who understands the nuances of insurance-backed investments can help you navigate these complexities.

Also, diversifying within insurance-backed investments can further mitigate risk. Rather than relying solely on a single type of product, you might consider a mix of annuities, life insurance policies with cash value benefits, and even long-term care insurance. This multifaceted approach helps balance the risk tailored to your financial situation and retirement objectives.

Meanwhile, don't overlook liquidity. Insurance products often come with certain restrictions on withdrawals and penalties for early surrender. It's vital to balance insurance-backed investments with other liquid assets within your portfolio. This ensures you have accessible funds for unforeseen expenses or financial opportunities that may arise.

Understanding your risk tolerance is another crucial element. While insurance-backed investments offer stability, they might not deliver the high returns possible with more aggressive investments. It's a trade-off between security and growth. Identifying your comfort level with risk will guide how much of your portfolio to allocate to these safer, albeit sometimes lower-yielding, options.

Lastly, always think of *insurance-backed investments* as pieces of a larger puzzle. They shouldn't represent your entire retirement strategy but rather complement it. Blending them with other investment vehicles like stocks, bonds, and real estate enables a diversified and well-rounded portfolio, enhancing your financial security.

In conclusion, balancing risk with insurance-backed investments is about more than just playing it safe. It's about smartly integrating stable, protective financial products into your broader retirement plan. Through thoughtful allocation, risk management, and a clear understanding of your financial goals, you can create a strategy that not only safeguards your assets but also supports your long-term well-being.

Each decision tailored to your unique situation can transform your retirement from a period of financial uncertainty to one of confident stability. In the next section, we'll delve into how to diversify your retirement portfolio using various insurance products, further extending this balanced approach.

Diversification with Insurance Products

This can be a game-changer when it comes to creating a robust retirement plan. By integrating various insurance products into your retirement strategy, you're adding layers of security and expanding the range of financial tools available to meet your long-term goals. Let's dive into the realm of diversification and understand how different insurance products can fortify your retirement planning.

When we talk about diversification, it's often in the context of investment portfolios—spreading assets to manage risk. However, diversification isn't limited to investments alone. Insurance products, like life insurance and annuities, can also play an essential role in helping mitigate risks and provide steady income. This multi-dimensional approach not only amplifies financial stability but also prepares you for unforeseen events.

Consider life insurance, for instance. While the primary purpose of life insurance is to provide a death benefit, it can also serve as an investment vehicle, especially permanent life insurance policies like whole or universal life. These policies accumulate cash value that can be borrowed against or withdrawn, offering a tax-advantaged source of funds that can support your retirement needs. Hence, incorporating life insurance into your retirement plan adds both protection and growth potential.

Annuities are another powerful tool in your diversification arsenal. They offer guaranteed income streams, which can be tailored to start at various points in your retirement. Whether you choose an immediate annuity that begins payouts right away or a deferred annuity that accumulates value over time before dispersing payments, these products help cover essential living expenses, decrease volatility impact, and ensure you're not solely dependent on market performance for your income.

Long-term care insurance is often overlooked but should be a vital component of a diversified retirement plan. The costs associated with prolonged medical care can be astronomical and erode your savings. By including long-term care insurance in your strategy, you're safeguarding your assets and alleviating the financial burden that would otherwise fall on yourself or your family. This insurance type specifically protects against the risk of large, unexpected healthcare costs, adding another layer of security.

The role of health insurance cannot be understated. Medicare, along with supplemental policies, ensures that routine and emergent healthcare needs are met without siphoning your retirement funds. But diversifying within health insurance options by exploring alternatives like Medicare Advantage plans or critical illness insurance could offer even more comprehensive coverage, tailored to your specific health profile and preference.

As you structure your diversification strategy, disability insurance should not be neglected. Retirement isn't immune to the risk of disability; it could occur at any time, jeopardizing your financial health. Long-term disability insurance offers a critical income replacement mechanism, ensuring that your retirement savings aren't depleted due to an unexpected disability.

Let's not forget liability insurance. Personal umbrella policies can provide extensive coverage over and above standard homeowners and auto insurance policies. These policies are crucial in protecting your assets from significant claims or lawsuits, which can seriously impact your financial stability. They add a protective layer, insulating your retirement funds from potential liabilities.

Your property and other valuable assets also require protection. Homeowners and auto insurance are standard, but ensuring you have sufficient coverage to account for all your properties and personal belongings is important. Specialized insurance policies can be aligned with your broader diversification strategy, securing investments like rental properties, vacation homes, or valuable collections. These measures extend the theme of diversification to tangible assets, protecting your portfolio comprehensively.

Balancing risk with insurance-backed investments can also yield significant benefits. Some life insurance policies and annuities offer investment components that allow for growth while providing a death benefit or guaranteed payouts. This creates a synergy between high-growth potential and risk reduction, creating a more balanced and resilient retirement portfolio.

One of the most significant benefits of diversifying with insurance products is the tax advantages they offer. Contributions and payouts from certain insurance types can be tax-free or tax-deferred, adding more value to your retirement funds. Understanding these tax advantages allows you to strategize your portfolio to maximize growth and minimize tax liabilities.

Diversification doesn't end at personal policies. Exploring group policies or employer-provided options can also broaden your insurance portfolio. Group policies usually come with lower premiums and might cover aspects that individual policies don't. As you transition into retirement, some of these group benefits may be portable, adding to the versatility and depth of your diversified approach.

So, how do you decide on the right mix of insurance products? It comes down to personalized planning and understanding your unique financial needs and risk tolerance. Working with a financial advisor who specializes in retirement planning can help tailor a diversification strategy that meets your goals and provides peace of reassurance.

To encapsulate, diversifying with insurance products provides a multi-faceted approach to retirement planning. It blends protection with investment, addresses various types of risks, and ensures a steady flow of income irrespective of market conditions. By leveraging the unique strengths of different insurance products, you create a comprehensive safety net that promises a secure and fulfilling retirement.

In the ever-changing landscape of retirement planning, diversification with insurance products is more than a strategy—it's a necessity for achieving and sustaining financial security throughout your golden years. Embrace this approach and forge a retirement plan that's not just resilient but also profoundly rewarding.

Chapter 11:
Tax Considerations for
Insurance in Retirement

As you navigate the labyrinth of retirement planning, understanding the tax implications of insurance products is paramount to maximizing your financial stability. While insurance policies often offer compelling tax advantages, such as tax-free death benefits and tax-deferred growth, it's crucial to be aware of how different retirement distributions are taxed. For instance, the proceeds from life insurance are typically free from federal income tax, providing a significant benefit to your beneficiaries. On the other hand, withdrawals from annuities can be subject to income tax, and the specifics vary depending on whether they are qualified or non-qualified contracts. Being proactive and informed about these tax considerations can help you make strategic decisions that preserve your wealth and ensure a smooth transition into your golden years. Understanding these nuances not only shields you from unexpected tax liabilities but also optimizes the economic efficiency of your retirement strategy, letting you enjoy the peace of mind that comes with a secure and well-planned financial future.

Tax Advantages of Insurance Policies

Tax Advantages of Insurance Policies are a crucial component for anyone looking to maximize their retirement planning strategy. Understanding these advantages can bring significant benefits, both in terms of financial security and peace of mind. Let's dive into the key benefits.

First and foremost, many life insurance policies offer tax-deferred growth on cash value accumulation. This means the money you contribute to your policy can grow without being subject to current income taxes. You're essentially allowing your investments within the policy to compound unhindered by annual tax liabilities.

Furthermore, the death benefit of a life insurance policy is generally paid out to beneficiaries tax-free. This can be a substantial boon for your loved ones, ensuring they receive the full sum you intended without the burden of federal income taxes. This feature makes life insurance an attractive tool for estate planning and wealth transfer.

For those holding permanent life insurance policies, you have the option to take out loans against the policy's cash value. These loans are often tax-free and can be used for various expenses, including funding your retirement. If managed properly, these loans do not even count as taxable income.

Another notable aspect is the ability to withdraw funds up to the amount of premiums paid, known as the "cost basis," without incurring tax penalties. This provides a unique layer of liquidity and flexibility during retirement, allowing for tax-free withdrawals if certain conditions are met.

In the realm of annuities, the tax benefits are equally compelling. Like permanent life insurance, annuities grow tax-deferred. Earnings accumulate without immediate tax implications, bolstering your retirement funds more efficiently over time. Taxes are only paid upon withdrawal, which can align with your retirement when you may be in a lower tax bracket.

Annuities also offer a strategic tool for income distribution. When set up appropriately, the payments from fixed and variable annuities can be structured to spread out your tax liability over many years. This structured payout can help mitigate the risk of large tax hits in any single year, aiding in more predictable financial planning.

Tax-advantaged retirement plans like Roth IRAs can also be strategically funded with life insurance proceeds. The tax-free death benefit provides an excellent source to fund Roth IRAs for your beneficiaries, allowing for further tax-free growth and distributions in their future.

There's also the consideration of avoiding probate. When designated as a beneficiary on insurance policies, you can keep these assets out of probate proceedings. This not only speeds up the distribution process to heirs but minimizes additional costs and taxes associated with probate.

Another often-overlooked advantage is the potential for tax deductions on long-term care insurance premiums. Depending on your age and policy specifics, these premiums might be deductible as medical expenses on your federal income tax return, offering some relief on out-of-pocket costs.

Life insurance policies can also be designed to fund tax-advantaged charitable contributions. By naming a charity as the beneficiary of your life insurance policy, you can provide significant support to the organization while avoiding estate and income taxes, creating a lasting legacy.

Incorporating these tax advantages smartly into your retirement plan isn't just about saving money; it's about optimizing your resources for a secure and fulfilling retirement. These financial techniques empower you to leverage the IRS rules in your favor, creating a well-rounded, tax-efficient retirement strategy.

Understanding the intersection of tax laws and insurance products may seem daunting, but it is essential to work with financial advisors who specialize in these areas. Their expertise ensures you maximize every possible tax advantage while maintaining a coherent and durable retirement plan.

Ultimately, the tax advantages of insurance policies give you more control over your financial destiny. They offer robust tools to manage your wealth, secure your family's future, and mitigate tax burdens, enabling a more predictable and serene retirement landscape.

Navigating the Tax Implications of Retirement Distributions

This can be a labyrinthine endeavor if you're not fully equipped with the right knowledge and tools. Retirement distributions, also known as withdrawals or rollovers from your retirement accounts, come with their unique set of rules and tax guidelines that can significantly affect the net amount you receive.

First, let's paint the broad strokes. When you start withdrawing money from your retirement accounts—tax-deferred accounts like traditional IRAs, 401(k)s, or pensions—the distributions are generally taxed as ordinary income. This means they'll hit your tax return just like your salary once did. Now, understanding this is crucial because your tax bracket may shift, affecting not just what you owe in taxes on those distributions but potentially other aspects of your financial life as well.

The timing of your distributions matters. The IRS has mandated that you start taking Required Minimum Distributions (RMDs) from most retirement accounts by April 1 of the year following the year in which you turn 72. Failing to take RMDs can result in hefty penalties—usually about 50% of the amount that should have been withdrawn. So, needless to say, it's a deadline worth noting on your calendar.

Strategizing these distributions can yield significant tax savings. Breaking up your withdrawals into smaller, more manageable chunks over several years, as opposed to large lump sums, can keep you in a lower tax bracket and reduce your overall tax liability. Balancing when and how much to withdraw can become a delicate dance, especially if you have multiple accounts.

Then, there are Roth IRAs. Unlike their traditional counterparts, Roth IRA distributions are typically tax-free, provided the account has been open for at least five years and you're above the age of 59½. Because you've already paid taxes on the money going into a Roth IRA, you can take it out without the tax hit—making Roth IRAs an excellent vehicle for tax-efficient withdrawals in retirement.

The taxation doesn't end with federal income taxes. Depending on where you live, state taxes might also come into play. Some states don't tax retirement income at all, while others will bite into your distributions just as they do with your regular income. Knowing your state's tax laws and planning accordingly can make a substantial difference.

Planning for Social Security benefits is another important aspect. Your retirement distributions could affect how much of your Social Security benefits are taxed. Up to 85% of your benefits could be subject to tax, depending on your total income and filing status. By managing your retirement distributions wisely, you can potentially minimize the tax impact on your Social Security benefits.

Converting traditional retirement accounts to Roth IRAs, known as a Roth conversion, can be an effective strategy. This involves paying taxes on the converted amount in the year of the conversion, but then enjoying tax-free withdrawals from the Roth IRA in the future. This strategy works best if you anticipate being in a higher tax bracket later or if you want to leave a tax-free inheritance to your heirs.

Charitable contributions can also offer tax advantages. If you're subject to RMDs but don't need the income, you can make a Qualified Charitable Distribution (QCD) directly from your IRA to a qualifying charity. A QCD can count towards your RMD for the year and isn't included in your taxable income, thereby reducing your tax liability.

Tax planning shouldn't be a do-it-yourself project. Having professionals in your corner—like a certified public accountant (CPA), a financial advisor skilled in retirement planning, or an estate lawyer—can ensure you're making the most tax-efficient decisions. An advisor can help you craft a distribution plan that aligns with both your financial needs and your long-term tax strategy.

Record-keeping is pivotal. Keep meticulous records of your distributions, conversions, and any charitable donations you make. Detailed documents ensure you're ready for tax season and protect you in case of an IRS audit. It's always better to have a well-organized paper trail that substantiates your tax planning efforts.

The tax landscape is ever-changing, with new laws and regulations potentially affecting your retirement strategy. Staying informed and periodically reviewing your financial and tax planning with a professional is crucial to adapt to these changes effectively.

Your retirement is meant to be enjoyed, not spent fretting over tax bills. Leveraging tax-advantaged strategies in your distributions will help you keep more of your money in your pocket, enabling you to enjoy the fruits of your labor more fully.

If you can map out your distribution strategy with foresight and professional advice, you'll be well on your way to a smooth, tax-efficient retirement. Embrace this process as a vital component of your broader retirement plan, and you'll find yourself more financially secure and confident in your golden years.

The goal here is not just to minimize taxes but to optimize your overall financial well-being. With intelligent planning and proactive measures, navigating the tax implications of retirement distributions becomes less daunting and more empowering.

Chapter 12:
A Guide to Estate Planning
with Insurance

When it comes to securing your legacy, estate planning with insurance is a game changer. This chapter highlights how insurance products can seamlessly integrate into your estate planning strategy, ensuring that your wealth is preserved and passed on efficiently. Insurance isn't just about providing a death benefit; it's about creating a solid framework for financial security that can span generations. From leveraging life insurance policies to fund trusts to using them for estate tax liquidity, you'll uncover innovative methods to safeguard your assets and provide for loved ones. In essence, through well-thought-out insurance strategies, you can establish a legacy that reflects your values and secures a stable future for your descendants. So, let's dive into the transformative power of insurance in estate planning, setting the stage for a legacy that endures.

Using Insurance Products to Create a Legacy

This topic is more than simply managing risks; it embodies your financial wisdom and provides a lasting benefit to the ones you love. If your aim is to not only secure your retirement but also leave behind a legacy that reflects your life's accomplishments and dreams for your family, insurance products can be powerful tools in your arsenal.

Life insurance, in particular, is often underappreciated in its ability to serve as a legacy-building tool. Whether you choose term life or permanent life insurance, each has the potential to offer a financial buffer for your descendents. With permanent life insurance, you get the added advantage of accumulating a cash value component that can be tapped into if unexpected needs arise during your lifetime. This dual advantage can be part of a strategic legacy plan.

The role of insurance in legacy planning isn't limited to just securing a lump sum payout. For example, policies can be structured to provide ongoing disbursements to beneficiaries, offering a steady income stream rather than a one-time windfall. This can be especially useful in ensuring that the money is used responsibly, providing long-term benefits rather than a short-term burst of spending.

Moreover, designating a life insurance policy to fund a trust can be a smart move. Trusts are an excellent way to manage and allocate assets according to a predefined plan. You can dictate the terms of the trust to specify how and when your beneficiaries receive the payouts, thereby maintaining a degree of control even after you're gone. This can be particularly useful when beneficiaries are minors or have specific needs that require ongoing support.

Another significant feature of certain insurance products is the ability to leverage them for estate tax planning. Estate taxes can significantly diminish the assets you plan to pass on to your heirs, but a life insurance policy, especially one held in an irrevocable life insurance trust (ILIT), can provide the liquidity needed to cover these taxes, ensuring that the bulk of your estate remains intact for your heirs.

It's also essential to think about charitable giving when considering your legacy. Life insurance can serve as a powerful vehicle for philanthropy. By designating a favorite charity as a beneficiary, you can create a lasting charitable legacy without affecting your family's financial security. Additionally, some policies allow you to assign a portion of the cash value to charitable organizations, enabling you to see the impact of your contributions during your lifetime.

Policy riders, such as the long-term care rider or disability waiver, can also add nuanced value to your legacy planning. These riders offer additional protection that ensures your policy remains in force even if unforeseen health issues arise. This not only preserves the benefit for your beneficiaries but also covers potential costs that might otherwise drain your estate.

In the realm of legacy planning, diversification is equally as vital. Combine different types of insurance products to balance liquidity, security, and growth. Using a mix of term, whole, and universal life insurance can help you optimize both your living benefits and the eventual legacy for your beneficiaries. Each type has its own set of advantages and understanding these can guide you toward a comprehensive legacy plan.

Insurance products are often seen through the lens of individual policies, but they can be more potent when viewed as part of an integrated strategy. For instance, synergizing life insurance with other investment vehicles like annuities can ensure a well-rounded approach. Annuities can offer you a predictable income during retirement, while life insurance secures the future for your heirs.

Another aspect to consider is the role of inflation. Over time, the purchasing power of money erodes, and this needs to be factored into your legacy planning. Policies that offer inflation protection riders can help ensure that your benefit retains its value, providing true financial security to your heirs in the future. Addressing inflation proactively can make a big difference in the long-term efficacy of your legacy planning.

It's equally important to review and adjust your policies periodically. Life changes, and so do your legacy goals. Births, deaths, marriages, and even divorces can affect beneficiary designations and the adequacy of coverage. A regular review ensures that your policies remain aligned with your intended legacy. Not doing so can lead to unintended consequences, causing more harm than good to your financial legacy.

Working with a professional advisor can provide invaluable insights into structuring your legacy. Advisors have the expertise to tailor strategies that incorporate various insurance products, trust arrangements, and tax considerations. Their role is to navigate the complexities of these components, crafting a legacy plan that aligns with your overall financial goals.

Transparency is equally vital when planning your legacy. Communicate your intentions with your beneficiaries. It helps in setting expectations and reduces potential conflicts or misunderstandings later on. Clear communication can also help your heirs understand and appreciate the value of the legacy you're leaving them, ensuring it's used wisely and according to your wishes.

Lastly, consider the emotional and ethical dimensions of your legacy. Employing insurance products to create a legacy isn't just about dollars and cents. It's about the values you wish to impart and the message you want to leave behind. The strategic use of insurance can reflect your life's values and priorities, providing a lasting tribute to your life's journey and the people you cared for.

Inheritance isn't merely a financial transaction; it's a narrative of love, foresight, and responsibility. By thoughtfully employing insurance products, you can weave a legacy that speaks volumes about who you were, your dreams for your loved ones, and the care with which you prepared for their future. Indeed, the thoughtful deployment of these tools can help you create a legacy that endures well beyond your lifetime.

Trusts and Insurance: Protecting Your Estate for Future Generations

Here, we combine two pivotal strategies to ensure your estate is safeguarded and that your beneficiaries are well-prepared for the future. A trust is a powerful tool in estate planning, and when coupled with the right insurance products, the potential to amplify protection and flexibility is unparalleled.

To start, let's demystify what a trust entails. A trust is a fiduciary arrangement that allows a third party, or trustee, to manage assets on behalf of beneficiaries. The core advantage of a trust is control; you can specify exactly how and when the assets pass to your heirs. This structured approach helps avoid probate, saving time and often, substantial legal costs.

Adding insurance into this mix isn't just a cherry on top—it's a smart move that can provide liquidity precisely when it's needed. For instance, life insurance policies can be set up to pay out directly into a trust, ensuring your heirs receive the benefits without the hassles and delays of probate. This immediate cash influx can cover estate taxes, alleviate debt, or fund education for your grandchildren.

When considering the types of trusts available, there are many to choose from, each serving a unique purpose. An irrevocable life insurance trust (ILIT) is especially pertinent. With an ILIT, you essentially remove the life insurance policy from your estate, which can have significant tax advantages. The proceeds from the policy don't get counted as part of your taxable estate, depriving the tax man of a portion of your legacy.

Another crucial aspect is asset protection. Creditors can't touch the contents of an irrevocable trust, making this a potent choice for safeguarding your estate. Combine this with a robust life insurance plan, and you create a nearly impenetrable wall of security, ensuring your assets pass on as you intended.

Moreover, trusts can be tailored to specific needs, such as a special needs trust, which ensures that a child or dependent with disabilities is financially supported without jeopardizing their eligibility for government benefits. Pairing this with a permanent life insurance policy can provide lifelong care long after you're gone.

Insurance also allows for greater flexibility in your estate planning. For example, term life insurance can be a temporary solution to ensure a trust is funded sufficiently until other investments mature. On the other hand, permanent life insurance policies can provide a guaranteed payout regardless of when the insured passes, aligning perfectly with the long-term benefits of a trust.

There's a scenario where using a trustee-designed insurance policy really shines. The trustee can use the insurance proceeds to buy out siblings' interests in a family business, thus avoiding forced sales and preserving the business for those family members who are involved in its operations. This can ensure the business remains intact, preventing discord and potentially destructive legal battles.

A significant benefit of this approach is also psychological—it offers peace of mind. Knowing your heirs and beneficiaries are cared for through a carefully structured blend of trusts and insurance policies provides comfort and assurance. It aligns with the very essence of responsible planning, ensuring that those you love are protected and provided for in the exact way you intend.

Crafting strategies that integrate both trusts and insurance also introduces a level of professional oversight that can be critical. Engaging financial advisors, tax professionals, and legal experts helps orchestrate this harmony, leveraging their expertise to fine-tune your plans. This professional guidance ensures compliance with ever-changing laws and regulations, safeguarding the integrity of your estate plan.

One salient point to remember is that this combined approach isn't just for the wealthy. Middle-income families can significantly benefit from this strategy, especially when it comes to ensuring that educational funds, medical expenses, or mortgage payments are enabled by structured insurance payouts managed within a trust.

Incorporating trusts and insurance offers an insurance-backed safety net that withstands life's uncertainties. With careful planning, clear instructions, and the right legal frameworks, you're building an enduring legacy that benefits your family for generations. This strategic approach allows for seamless transitions, equitable distributions, and above all, the preservation of what you've worked so hard to achieve.

The beauty of weaving together trusts and insurance lies in the customization. Whether it's through staggered insurance benefits released at milestones such as graduations or structured trust disbursements upon achieving predetermined family goals, the level of personalization is immense. This ensures that your legacy is not only protected but also perpetuated in a manner aligned with your values and objectives.

Ultimately, the convergence of trusts and insurance encapsulates a robust estate planning philosophy. It transcends merely protecting assets; it embodies a comprehensive strategy to fortify your financial legacy, providing reassurance that your family's future remains secure, come what may. The collaborative synergy between these elements underscores a visionary approach to financial maturity, giving your life's achievements a lasting impact.

Chapter 13:
Ensuring a Secure and Sustainable Retirement

We've traveled through a landscape of insurance products, from life insurance and annuities to long-term care and disability insurance. Each of these tools serves its own unique purpose, yet all have a common goal: to safeguard your retirement. But identifying these tools is just the start. Integrating them into a strategy that both protects and empowers you requires a thoughtful and comprehensive approach.

First and foremost, let's recognize that there is no one-size-fits-all solution. Your financial needs and goals are distinct. They evolve over time, influenced by market conditions, health changes, and family dynamics. The strategy we've discussed is dynamic, adaptable, and most importantly, personalized. Keep this in mind as you revisit and refine your retirement plan over the years.

One key to ensuring a secure retirement is diversification. We've touched upon how different insurance products can complement each other, creating a safety net that mitigates risks while offering growth opportunities. It's crucial not to rely solely on one type of insurance or investment. Diversification can protect against uncertainties, offering more peace of mind as you transition through various stages of retirement.

Additionally, the role of professional guidance can't be overstated. While this book provides a robust framework, consulting with financial advisors, insurance agents, and tax professionals can add nuanced insights tailored to your unique situation. These experts can help interpret the complexities and make informed decisions that align with your overall retirement objectives.

It's also important to be proactive in periodic reviews of your retirement plan. Life is unpredictable; changes in health, family, and even legislation can impact your financial standing. Scheduled reviews offer an opportunity to adjust your strategies, ensuring they remain relevant and effective. Just as you wouldn't set a course on a long road trip without checking in periodically via GPS, your retirement plan needs regular check-ins.

One of the most empowering aspects of utilizing insurance products in retirement planning is the control they offer. Whether it's the guaranteed income from annuities, the protection against unforeseen health costs from long-term care insurance, or the legacy planning through life insurance, these products provide options that keep you in the driver's seat. Retirement should be about enjoying the fruits of your labor, not stressing over financial instability.

Legacy planning deserves special mention. Many retirees are not only thinking about their immediate needs but also about the financial well-being of their descendants. Life insurance and estate planning tools can create a lasting impact, providing for future generations and ensuring your values and wishes are honored. A well-thought-out legacy plan can instill a sense of purpose and fulfillment as you witness the positive effects of your planning unfold.

Let's not forget about the ever-important aspect of tax considerations. The tax landscape can significantly influence the net benefits of different insurance products, thus impacting your overall retirement strategy. Ensuring you understand and optimize the tax advantages offered by various insurance products will allow for maximum efficiency and the preservation of your hard-earned savings.

The synergy between investments and insurance is another cornerstone of a sustainable retirement strategy. With the right balance, you can achieve both security and growth. While insurance products provide a safety net, investment strategies drive the potential for wealth accumulation. This balanced approach ensures that you're covered for immediate needs while also growing your assets for future requirements.

To create a robust strategy, don't overlook the importance of property and casualty insurance. Protecting your tangible assets—your home, car, and other valuable possessions—ensures that an unexpected event doesn't erode your financial stability. Comprehensive coverage under an umbrella policy can add that extra layer of security.

Moreover, the integration of Social Security benefits with other retirement income sources is crucial. Timing your Social Security claims strategically and aligning them with your insurance benefits can maximize your overall retirement income. This coordinated approach can enhance your financial independence, allowing you to enjoy retirement without constant financial worries.

The psychological benefits of a well-structured retirement plan can't be ignored. Knowing that you have a safety net in place can eliminate the mental burden of financial uncertainty, allowing you to focus on enjoying your retirement. It grants you the freedom to pursue hobbies, travel, and spend quality time with loved ones.

Ultimately, a secure and sustainable retirement boils down to thoughtful planning, regular reviews, and a balanced approach. This book has aimed to arm you with the knowledge and tools to navigate the complexities of retirement planning. By using insurance products judiciously, you can build a retirement that is not only financially secure but also enriching and fulfilling.

As you move forward, remember that every step you take towards securing your retirement is an investment in your future well-being. There's great wisdom in being prepared. Embrace the journey with confidence, knowing that you have laid down a strong foundation for a fulfilling and secure retirement.

Here's to a future of financial stability, peace of mind, and the freedom to live your retirement years to the fullest!

Glossary of
Insurance Terms for Easy Reference

As you explore the world of insurance and its role in retirement planning, it can be helpful to have a quick reference guide to some of the most commonly used terms. Here's a comprehensive glossary to help you understand the terminology and make informed decisions.

Actuarial

Relating to statistical calculations, especially of life expectancy and risk, often used in the underwriting and pricing of insurance policies.

Annuitant

The person who receives the payments from an annuity. Typically, the annuitant is also the policyholder.

Annuity

A financial product that pays out a fixed stream of payments to an individual, primarily used as an income stream for retirees.

Beneficiary

The person or entity designated to receive the death benefit from a life insurance policy or an annuity contract.

Cash Value

The amount available in cash upon the policyholder's voluntary termination of a permanent life insurance policy before it becomes payable by death or maturity.

Claim

A request made by the insured or the insured's beneficiary for payment of benefits provided by an insurance policy.

Coverage

The scope of protection provided under an insurance policy, typically noted in the form of coverage limits, inclusions, and exclusions.

Deductible

The amount the insured must pay out-of-pocket before the insurance company pays its share of a covered claim.

Death Benefit

The amount paid to a beneficiary upon the death of the insured, typically associated with life insurance policies.

Disability Insurance

Insurance designed to provide income replacement in the event the insured is unable to work due to disability.

Endorsement

An amendment or addition to the original insurance policy, which can alter coverage or terms.

Face Amount

The amount stated on the face of the insurance policy that will be paid upon death or maturity, also known as the policy limit.

Leverage

In the context of insurance, using borrowed capital for investment, expecting that the profits made will be greater than the interest payable.

Liability Insurance

Coverage that protects against claims alleging that one's negligence or inappropriate action resulted in bodily injury or property damage.

Long-Term Care Insurance

Insurance designed to cover the costs of long-term care services, such as in-home care, nursing homes, and assisted living facilities.

Medigap

Supplemental insurance for Medicare beneficiaries to cover gaps in original Medicare plans, such as copayments, coinsurance, and deductibles.

Premium

The amount paid for an insurance policy, usually on a monthly, quarterly, or annual basis.

Rider

An additional provision added to an insurance policy that provides extra benefits or amends the coverage.

Surrender Value

The amount the policyholder is entitled to receive if they terminate the policy before maturity or the insured event occurs.

Term Life Insurance

Life insurance that provides coverage at a fixed rate of payments for a limited period, or term. After the term expires, the policyholder can typically renew for another term or convert to permanent coverage.

Underwriting

The process of evaluating the risk of insuring a person or asset and determining the premium that needs to be charged to accept that risk.

Variable Annuity

An annuity contract where the payout amounts vary based on the performance of the investments chosen by the policyholder.

Whole Life Insurance

A type of permanent life insurance that provides coverage for the life of the insured and includes a cash value component.

- Whole Life Insurance is known for its guaranteed death benefit and fixed premiums.
- Policyholders can borrow against the cash value component.

This glossary is designed to be a handy resource as you delve deeper into the various insurance products that can play a crucial role in your retirement planning. Understanding these terms can empower you to make informed decisions that will secure your financial future and provide peace of mind.

Appendix A:
Insurance Planning Worksheets
and Checklists

Achieving a secure retirement involves careful planning and thorough understanding of various insurance products. This appendix provides you with useful worksheets and checklists to help you navigate insurance choices and integrate them effectively into your retirement plan. Think of this as your practical toolkit for taking actionable steps toward a financially secure future.

Insurance Needs Assessment Worksheet

Before diving into specific insurance products, it's essential to assess your overall insurance needs. This worksheet will help you evaluate your current coverage, identify gaps, and determine the types of insurance that are best suited for your retirement plan.

1. Current Insurance Policies:

   - Life Insurance Policy 1: _____

   - Life Insurance Policy 2: _____

   - Health Insurance: _____

   - Long-Term Care Insurance: _____

   - Disability Insurance: _____

   - Property and Casualty Insurance: _____

2. Expected Post-Retirement Risks:

- Healthcare Expenses
- Long-Term Care Costs
- Loss of Income Due to Disability
- Estate Taxes and Fees
- Liability Risks

3. Gaps in Coverage:

- Areas where you lack sufficient coverage: _____
- Additional coverage needed: _____

4. Action Plan:

- Policies to review for changes or upgrades: _____
- New policies to consider: _____

Life Insurance Checklist

Life insurance can serve multiple needs in retirement, from providing a safety net for loved ones to being a tool in your estate planning strategy. Use this checklist to ensure you've covered all the bases.

- Compare term vs. permanent life insurance options.
- Determine the death benefit needed to cover expenses and leave a legacy.
- Review and update beneficiaries regularly.
- Assess whether life insurance can be used for estate planning purposes, such as paying estate taxes or providing liquidity.
- Consider leveraging life insurance policies to supplement retirement income.

Annuities and Income Planning Worksheet

Annuities can provide a stable income stream in retirement. This worksheet helps you identify which types of annuities might suit your needs and how to integrate them into your income plan.

1. Identify Income Gaps:

   - Current retirement income sources (e.g., Social Security, pensions): _____

   - Estimated monthly expenses in retirement: _____

   - Income gap that needs to be filled: _____

2. Types of Annuities to Consider:

   - Immediate Annuities: _____

   - Deferred Annuities: _____

   - Fixed Annuities: _____

   - Variable Annuities: _____

   - Indexed Annuities: _____

3. Annuity Integration Plan:

   - Annuity type chosen: _____

   - Monthly income expected: _____

   - Timing of annuity payouts: _____

Long-Term Care Insurance Checklist

Long-term care insurance is crucial for covering the high cost of long-term care services. Use this checklist to determine the key factors to consider when selecting a long-term care policy.

   - Assess the potential need for long-term care based on family history and personal health.

- Calculate the estimated cost of long-term care services in your area.

- Review policy options for coverage amount, benefit period, and elimination period.

- Understand policy exclusions and limitations.

- Consider inflation protection options to ensure your benefit keeps up with rising costs.

Health Insurance Options for Retirees Worksheet

Healthcare can be a significant expense in retirement. This worksheet helps you outline your health insurance options and plan for associated costs.

1. Current Health Insurance Coverage:

   - Medicare: Part A, Part B, Part D: _____

   - Medicare Supplement (Medigap) Policy: _____

   - Employer-sponsored retiree health plan: _____

   - Other health insurance: _____

2. Future Health Insurance Needs:

   - Gaps in current coverage: _____

   - Additional coverage needed: _____

   - Estimated out-of-pocket healthcare costs: _____

3. Health Insurance Action Plan:

   - Review and compare Medicare Advantage plans

   - Consider purchasing or upgrading a Medigap policy

   - Evaluate eligibility for Medicaid or other assistance programs

Regular Review and Update Checklist

As life changes, so too should your insurance coverage. Here's a checklist to ensure you're regularly reviewing and updating your insurance policies to suit your evolving needs.

- Review all insurance policy details annually.
- Update beneficiaries as life changes (e.g., marriage, divorce, birth of a child).
- Assess any new health developments that might affect your insurance needs.
- Adjust coverage for any major life events (e.g., retirement, downsizing your home).
- Ensure that premiums are still manageable within your retirement budget.

Using these worksheets and checklists, you can navigate the complexities of insurance planning with greater confidence and clarity. Take the time to sit down, fill them out, and consult with a financial advisor if needed. Your future self will thank you for the diligent planning and thoughtful preparation you undertake today.

Online Review Request for This Book

We'd really appreciate it if you could take a moment to share your thoughts and experience with this book by leaving an online review,

as it helps others on their journey to secure and strategic retirement planning.

www.ingramcontent.com/pod-product-compliance
Lightning Source LLC
Chambersburg PA
CBHW030530210326
41597CB00014B/1099